Futz
and
What Came After

●

ROCHELLE OWENS

Futz

and

What Came After

WITH AN INTRODUCTION BY

JEROME ROTHENBERG

RANDOM HOUSE

New York

Library of Congress Catalog Card Number: 68–18263

Typography by Kenneth Miyamoto
Manufactured in the United States of America by
The Colonial Press Inc., Clinton, Massachusetts

I'm easy to understand! I'm yielding! I'm humble! I can hum! I can chirp! Look! I am no Emperor! No tyrannical fierce King! I am not dangerous!

He Wants Shih

Introduction

•

I WASN'T THERE when tragedy was goat-song, were you? But I have a hunch that with all the great ones it persists, an animal presence thumping and throbbing 'neath the surface, then truly breaking out. That's when the hair rises in all the glory and wonder of theater and the poet's art. Laughter fills us, but our eyes are on the knife above the goat's throat, or on the priest's mouth stuffed with macaronis turning into blood, or on the hairy feet of a crazed Eastern saint spinning off into dark circles inside some northern mind, or on those shadows in the barn of Cyrus Futz that drive a culture mad. Rochelle Owens has caught hold of a truth about our nature, and she rides it through these plays, creating a new theater as she goes and a world of her own. Rochelle Owens' "world" and her theater of *impulse!* But don't be fooled into thinking that "you" aren't part of it. "You" are and "I" am too: looking back at history with her own eyes until we realize that the world she's showing us is in us all.

Her first play, *Futz*, announces the theme: man as animal, the talking, questioning and self-destructive animal—cruel—one of all our dreams and fears. But it is man too who makes love, creates it and gives it its name. Still, perversity remains love's sister, and cruelty is the image of love in

vii

the mind's steamed mirror. None of it comes easy, for man learns to lie (both to himself and others) even as he learns to speak. All Cretans are liars, said Epimenides the Cretan, and the curtain of darkness fell down.

So there's "love" to begin with—that love which, wrote Dante, "is the seed of every virtue in us, and of every action deserving punishment." In *Futz* the drives, open or hidden, are sexual (virtuous too—and oh so cruel), and Futz himself, who cries at his tormentors, "I love Amanda [the sow] because she's good," emerges finally as man-of-values, defender of all the grubby wonders of our flesh. Goat-song or pig-song, he is the old animal god who dies to save the secrets of the soul. *Yus Yus Yus oooooooooooinkh,* Futz bellows *in extremis,* and his murderers ("mean folks" who, "wanting to love the animals the way I do . . . hate my face"), pig-like, respond, *YUS Yus Yus.*

The cries and the wild-words of *Futz* inform the later plays too—the "what-came-after" of the present volume—only here (very naturally) the range of drives and longings is expanded, and the plot (as they say) begins-to-thicken. Sex, hunger, flight, aggression, the need to rule and to be ruled, to love and devour, all these are now in operation—and the struggle they engender is seen also as one between races, cultures and nations. But there is more than thesis writing here, because the playwright, as *poet,* has allowed herself the danger of an involvement in the very madness she portrays. She has remembered too that poetry and theater flourish at the extremes of our human and animal natures, where even the unlikely is true. For with all her mad and maddeningly believable histories and geographies —those Greenlands and Africas and Istanbouls and Asias of the mind—this is no mere exoticism she's serving us. To put it mildly (and not to repeat again the list of modern

Introduction

torture chambers from Auschwitz to Vietnam), there is nothing her white goddess, Beclch, does that the collectivity (all of us, whether we like it or not) hasn't done already in the course of this or any other century. Do away with cruelty and the destructive instincts of the trapped animal, and these plays will be obsolete in their themes; until then, we need poets like this one, to fight cruelty in its own terms and language, to expose it with all that laughter and horror that have been the tools of the great comic poets from Aristophanes to Ben Jonson to (why not just say it?) Rochelle Owens.

JEROME ROTHENBERG
New York City

CONTENTS

Introduction
by Jerome Rothenberg
vii

Futz
1

The String Game
31

Beclch
71

Istanbul
155

Homo
197

Futz

FUTZ was first presented for one performance on October 10, 1965, at the Tyrone Guthrie Workshop at the Minnesota Theatre Company. It was then presented by the LaMama Troupe on March 1, 1967, at The LaMama Theatre in New York City, with the following cast:

(*In order of appearance*)

NARRATOR	Beverly Atkinson
CYRUS FUTZ	John Bakos
MAJORIE SATZ	Beth Porter
OSCAR LOOP	Seth Allen
BILL MARJORAM	Michael Warren Powell
KEEPER	Peter Craig
ANN FOX	Mari-Claire Charba
SHERIFF TOM SLUCK	Peter Craig
FATHER SATZ	Rob Thirkield
MOTHER SATZ	Mari-Claire Charba
BROTHER NED SATZ	Victor LiPari
MRS. LOOP	Marilyn Roberts
WARDEN	Peter Craig
SUGFORD	Michael Warren Powell
BUFORD	Peter Craig

Music and direction by Tom O'Horgan
Set designed by Saito
Lighting by Laura Rambaldi
Technical Assistant Howard Vishinsky

3

Now concerning the things whereof ye wrote unto me:
It is good for a man not to touch a woman.

I Corinthians 7:1

SCENE 1

NARRATOR Let's give it a strange passion to a story, some handyman handy in the barns with animals—"someone to watch over him"—somethings, the udders of the moo-moo especially. No stupid pretty girl to rely on him, like a home-made stunt between his feet, to knock up his knees—bad onions—spoiling him eternally. Small fetid room, obvious barn-like, but still a small room with lots of oily automobile rags and other signs of the terrible city existence, brewed still more stinky with the worst the country has to offer—dead grassy worms; horses' shit; small portions of a moldy outhouse; summer brooms; women's drawers; rubber suits for working in the water; etc. Anything you can think up naturally. Cy Futz, a Scandinavian sort of big fellow, wearing new dungarees, bell bottom, they could be overalls, comes in filled with a sexual dream; it does not bear in the least to anything real in terms of yours or Cy's world. It's pure sickness, but in its pureness it's a truth. Sitting down on a wet broken step, he says:

CY o the cow's tits are bigger and I know it's wrong, but young uns never know the difference between an animal's or a woman's hip bones, so soft like my socks, fresh washed

5

like new kids's hoofs. O I could sing. OOOOOoooOOOOO-
oooooOOOO LooLoooooooooLOOOOOOO Looy LOOY
LOY LORD LORD I LOVE YOU GOD. And I have no
hate for anybody, but wanting to love the animals the
way I do. *They,* mean folks hate my face. I turn around
the corners and make fun on their asses, no tickle does
theirs feel like my own good one as I sing tears in the
sow's belly. With their fried eggs for wives, they know
no song.

NARRATOR   Again he sings his ooo's and looooo's intermin-
gled with a belch and a mock fart and ending with three
very loud "Lords." All the time he's buttering his wrists
with his red hands, making bird and other noises, he is
very excited and seems absolutely certain to explode all
his love or whatever over the world which is the room
where he is in now. Now she comes in, Miss Majorie
Satz, about twenty-seven years old, tall with a square
worldly, insulted once maybe, body. Her coarse red hair
is combed up in a sophisticated way which is sweetly
silly in retrospect to her food-stained gingham, typical
farm girl get-up.

MAJORIE   Hello Bastady man. Yus big man-bloke, I missed
you at the greengrocer, yus said that you would come,
yus said so, and I painted my big toe too for yu. (*Giggling*) Yu man-bloke, old Swede man.

NARRATOR   Cyrus is looking at her and is vexed at her,
probably Cy was always squinnied by her, probably
because she obviously is a woman in the very dreamy
sensual way which he only wants his animals to be.
Gentle sick man he is. He hoots at her.

CY   Hallas Majy Ya French dancer! You woman of ten
beds and manure heaps, yus stinking human woman with
only cat-mouths for tits and a baby-paw for your arse.
I did not want to see you, you told me a foul story the

last time that I saw you. Not again mind you do I want that shit! Always you are pretending to be my friend and better yet a hole for me to dive in, but I'd rather sink my pick in turd, cleaner my Lord more than you Maj! Nahhh! I don't want no sow with two feet but with four! Them repeats true things with their grunts not like you human-daughter.

NARRATOR Majorie moves backwards and starts to hum the French anthem.

MAJORIE I'll pick up my skirt right now if yu want. I'll get on my heels and elbows, old farmer, yus not so old yu know only forty, there are whut's younger men than yu who'd like to take me to a movie, strongir and slimmir than yu, so why make me hurt your chest—an' don't I buy you fodder for your sick love, Amanda the sow, so she could be a better one for yu? Even I know, who likes yu, how bud it is to sleep with a pig! Unnatural, like in the Bible, it's piggish—that's where the word comes from yus know piggish—from a pig yugh yugh sooo evil. Yu smell so baad it is no joke—

CY Go forget about it and your cheeks won't be nervous —put your nose out of my business, disgusting girl. I like Amanda because she's good. Pig or not. And I don't stink that's your lie—any much more than you or the boys that take you in the fields.

MAJORIE (*Hatefully*) That's your awn dirtty story 'nd it maks me nasty towards yu—I can't feel bad for your dread and doom—yu sleep with the unimals bitter bitter unholy unholy.

NARRATOR Cy pushes her from behind, then stoops and picks up a dirty broom, begins to sweep her flanks with a mock lust, also singing a very low song in a Celtic tune. She covers her ears and shrieks.

MAJORIE   Yeeeiiiiiey Oyu Big man-bloke!

NARRATOR   He snaps her rope belt with his left hand and slaps her face (not hard)* with the right. He pushes her ahead of him and they both go behind the half-rotten wall which was once an old outhouse.

(*Animal grunts sound and the lights are dimmed*)

SCENE 2

NARRATOR   Look at the old rotten wall—behind it, here are Cyrus and Maj and yugch! a sow. Amanda! The animal that's sure to steal forever Cy's heart (never to marry) yus, her, Maj, sweet flower, woman with a wholesome grin, and no hair on the chin, sallow woman with a cantaloupe seed in her belly and toes that are canary yellow. Ooopph.

(NARRATOR *pushes his hands in a cup form and feeds the sounds of grunts and human voice to the audience*)

MAJORIE   Pechhh *so* indecent, I'd live in shame if the village ever knew what I'd done.

CY   Fahhh my woman the people need never know what you done, anyways they would want the full freedom to be able to do what you done. Girl, peachy sweet currant stop being afraid, even the sow won't tell!

NARRATOR   Maj tears, she's sore afraid.

---

* Stage directions are either performed by the actors or verbalized by the narrator. This is left to the decision of the director.

MAJORIE   Yu make it wus tan it is mentionin' the pig—she does not know anyting about it, and she did not feel soft like you said but like an old razor on my feet. O o o so indecent I am, and now the filty dreams 'ill come. O Gods help meee that we shoulda both laid with a sow.

NARRATOR   Maj carries about awhile with hands scratching out her Lord from the sky, pushing him into her soul trying to wring his sweat from the skinny body, trying hard hard to have his water wash the dinny sin from her wretched body. Lust for animals is like a run in spring rain. (Sniggle) Lewd lewd, foosh foosh, and she calls on all the idols and the true god to make the slop go away.

CY   Now fish stop, stop fish, nobody knows and the pig won't tell.

MAJORIE   Stop stop stop! Yus mean rat, your modern sin has killed me!

CY   Isn't no modern sin, old as your Bible, lay down with a calf somebody did and did get no punishment from God, like your village will give you. Cluck, if you don't stop your sirens blowing, shit your mouth up Majorie, you're makin' me sound funny in my own ears and I have faith for my love of the animals with hoofs and corncob appitite, can't you really see—it is no wrong. They laugh more real than the mayor and your mother. Brooey to the devil for the bad conscience you feel, say phat phat to it. It don't pay.

MAJORIE   Your diggnitty is like sloppy ole shoes, but good luck to me, soon as I get away from evil—never again. Os Os never agin piggiying myself like that.

NARRATOR   She gets up from the bed of wet paper and rags, smoothing her clothes and wrapping her hair in her fists.

Cy watches her with pickles in his eyes. He spys the pig and on the knees and hands jerks towards her, sticking his fingers out like stone worms, his tongue lolls like mice in his mouth, he sticks his leg out, banging his shoe on the pig's ass (not cruelly though) just enough to make the animal turn and be conscious of him, for in that white-flesh no-blood brain she remembers pleasure. And she backs towards him you know and he grabs her body. Maj is watching with bloody senses, then tears out shrieking.

SCENE 3

NARRATOR   In an old-fashioned prison cell with the traditional water pot, hammock, etc., two men are talking (O everything is the same with these two as with a hundred other yolts). The jailbird, Oscar Loop, is skinny and wears the prison suit like he was a fallen priest, the other man is Bill Marjoram, squat, strong, sweaty and typical in work clothes, fat shoes, etc., how can well I go describing on?

LOOP   O breakfast is not much, I mean breakfast is not much, two pieces of bread, glass of water and a sausage, not real you know, something to think about anyway, sometimes I think like a motherless child, I mean take the tiny spices out of the sausage and grow them like small insects, I mean if they get watered and sun on them they might get life and then they'd be like insects.

BILL   Shut up, Loop! Stupid, talking 'bout insex and maybe hanging tomorra! Your riddles too! Make me sick.

LOOP   Listen, they would be spice insects, so you could eat them—they would even be medicinal, cure a palsy help-fully, jerk a dead newborn back to life. O I hope it would do all those things.

BILL Shut up, Loop! I said. Stupid. Don't you know you gonna die?

LOOP I mean a dead newborn could have been Mozart— I care in a great many ways for life, that's why the good sausage seed-spice might work (*Whispers*) without the evil eye, I bet Siva would help me, Siva is beautiful with her lovely hands, she's picked the mosquitoes out of my head. I've read greatly about her.

BILL You keep blabbing on 'nd on 'bout things that don't stop you from dying!

LOOP How do you know? What makes you be so sure? Anything cun help a man maybe, a rock hit a devil in the Bibledays and a devil sucked out the blood of the thrower of that rock in hell. Somebody made that devil draw out all the blood in the man. Hmmmmmmmmmmmmmmmm I'll have to write that on the sausage. Mustn't forgit all the marvelous thoughts I git lately.

BILL Mavilous thoughts my foot! Swear you're gonna hang on Monday. Man, think, Loop! Think! Whut did you do?

LOOP Whut did I do? Flah! A woman saw me, she bought me a mitten, tole me to put it on, said that the feeling would come through better. She looked like Mary in a story, but not the Lord's mother you know. No she looked like the whore. But then like him I changed her.

BILL Whut do you mean, changed her! Speak it up truthfully. You killed her!

LOOP I made her fall asleep on the ground. Put a bad blueberry in her mouth, Satan was a grub, and when he got inside of her he ate her innards out but that was God's wish.

NARRATOR Loop is smiling like a good king.

BILL How did she die? And if it's too bad a story, you bitter not tell it in your crazy way. Tell me how you killed the girl, nobody dies with fruitbugs, tell it sound and real.

NARRATOR Now there are keys and chains sounds, the prison keeper comes in and Loop, eyes frightened, begins to stretch. He is afraid that he has been heard.

(*Everybody cringes*)

LOOP I mean to say that what I tole Bill wasn't all so. (*Points to the keeper and ropes his arm toward himself*) You come here, guard, O I'm gonna tell you how I killed the girl, but in the beginning. Hoos! In the beginning was purity, and cleanliness was a big garter belt.

NARRATOR The keeper is sniffing in his giggles, feeling his bone, trying to see garter belts.

KEEPER Tell us what happened and maybe you can get a reprieve, hhah ha ha ha hiss— Did you put the garter belt 'round her small throat?

LOOP I met Ann Fox in the greengrocer's. I saw her skirt swing frisky, and I knew that her father was a good farmer and Baptist. I knew that everybody in the village liked that family. And no young fella would treat her disrespectfully. I could not just get married to a girl, without her being like Ann, I knew that I wouldn't get married and be normal—so I asked her out, and she went with me, she said she liked the smell of leather. You know I have a good leather belt and jacket that a handcrafts woman sent me. Well Ann liked that jacket, she said she'd take it from me when I was asleep. Sometimes I think she meant it too. Her father was a rich man, he could buy her all the leather clothes she wanted but she'd say she wanted my jacket too. Well I'd get mad thinking about it, though I knew too that she was playing. But I took her one night near the field where Cy Futz's barn is and we horseplayed a little bit, nothing but some hunky-punk.

SCENE 4

NARRATOR   A small dark field, nighttime, a blanket on the grass, a leather jacket spread perfectly out. Oscar Loop and Ann Fox are sitting opposite each other cross-legged.

LOOP   Little good cat, ooph you knock my eyes out of my head, you're so pretty.

NARRATOR   He sticks out his forefinger and strokes her nose.

ANN   Buford Skark says I'm pretty too, too bad to mention another fella? You both think the same, that I'm pretty.

NARRATOR   Loop hops on his knees hooping himself toward her (if it's possible lights should shine green on top of his hair).

LOOP   Little rat stop thinkin' of other men! Dogs 'ill crawl up your back if you do.

NARRATOR   He puts his hands on her hips and she falls at him laughing. They both move at each other like beach balls. Her foot catches in the jacket and he pushes at her ankle with two hands. She meanly slams her shoe into the precious leather.

LOOP   Crazy rich girl cut that out!

ANN   Hang it!

LOOP   Whut d'yu mean hang it! Have respect for a man's garment. I wear that on Sunday!

ANN On Sunday the people laugh at you too just like on Monday. Ooooobles you're serious, so, so serious. Why'nt you kiss me? I'm a girl.

LOOP I I I will kiss you—I would like to learn to dance, so that I can go with you to fancy places.

NARRATOR She moves her hip closer to his and takes his hand laying it on her stomach. He grabs her mightily and they kiss.

ANN I hear something, is it my head? There are crazy bees inside of it, you kiss crazy. (*Sounds, like those of an animal in heat, are heard*) Listen—I hear grunts! And I think someone cussing. Don't it sound strange?

LOOP Yus, I hear them too. Don't know why somebody should beat their animals. Terrible to do that—I would never do that.

NARRATOR Loop and Ann move very close to where the noises come from. Futz's barn. The barn is not seen though. The noise is a human and animal one. And both people are dumbstruck at what in all heaven's holy name is happening. Something equally weird is happening to Loop; he looks insane. He pushes himself at Ann and starts to pummel her, his voice is croaky.

LOOP Gonna rid the place of evil, gonna make you sleep a long time till your soul becomes clean.

ANN (*She screams*) Stop it stop it! Let me be.

NARRATOR She tries to get away but he drags her around in a small circle.

LOOP Gonna bury you in that evil dress, stink will in a hundred years be covered up by the sweet grass, hell isn't as bad as a whoring girl. May your father and mother not mourn you too long.

14

NARRATOR   Ann cries in soulful anguish. Loop drags her off.
He comes back in terribly bloody clothes and sits cross-
legged in the moony night. The animal sounds are louder
but he shows no life, just sits with his arms folded and the
hands covering his eyes. Then he slowly takes off his
shoes and with a monkey's grace raises his feet to his nose
and whiffs deeply.

SCENE 5

NARRATOR   Cy Futz's barn again just like in the beginning.
Cy is sitting with his kneebones high like the two hemi-
spheres. The pig Amanda is sleeping on her side.

CY   Flahfy Amanda ya faymale! Four ugly legs yu got, Zeus
wot hams. Lucky luck that I'm in love with you otherwise
you'd be hanging in my pantry. Heccchhhhchehehe when
you're old you'll be sitting in my granny's rockin' chair
readin' the Bible. Amanda you are of the world, known
two kinds of male animals, pig and man! Sow I know you
love me but I wonder whether you'd rather be with your
own kind? Piglets I can't give you you know though I am
a healthy man.

NARRATOR   Cy licks his hands passionately and praises God
for making him a husbandman. Silent is his worship but
the world enters his barn now. Bill Marjoram and the
Sheriff Tom Sluck, slowly they go up to him. Futz yawns
one eye open.

MARJORAM   There's the creep!

SLUCK   Y'all be quiet now.

MARJORAM   Quiet in hell, the biggest sinner in the world is
here. If we weren't fair he'd be dead now by our own
hands.

CY   I'd break them off like they were rabbits' necks.

SLUCK   Nothing is really proven yet. There will be justice.

MARJORAM   Men can make men insane!

SLUCK   Nothing is really proven yet.

MARJORAM   He drove a fella wacky!

CY   Fitz on you both boys! I know no man well enough to make him nuts. Tell me who's crazy?

SLUCK   A man's in jail now for murdering a girl, he killed because he saw something very evil.

CY   Very sad thing. But there's lotsa evil here in the world.

MARJORAM   You're the satan here in our village!

CY   I'm not anybody's keeper. I'm never near anybody. Except when they come here to see me. I just work on my little plot of land raisin' vegetables for me and my pig. What sort of evil could I have done?

NARRATOR   Cy plays a tom-tom with his feet, and salutes the sun. This is done subtly, the men not being aware of the ritual. Lord these two are blind!

SLUCK   The man who murdered an innocent girl says he did it because he was under an influence, a spell he says, because he's a simple man. Now Mr. Futz I'm going to be blunt. People say here that you are an unnatural man.

CY   Am I?

SLUCK   Well, aren't you?

MARJORAM   Gods he bangs pigs!

CY   I never do. Why my mother didn't bring me up like that. I'm a Bible man.

SLUCK If you're not serious you better become it. Very many people talk about your way.

CY They're all wrong Mr. Sluck. An animal is something to care about, not to commiteth a sin with. Soos!

MARJORAM See what he says! Soos!

SLUCK Soos! Soos! What does it mean?

MARJORAM It means he be guilty and pulling our feet.

CY Why why I never would go with an animal! I'm a village man and the sun is good on me, why I say that fellow has a devil in his head.

(*He points at* MARJORAM)

MARJORAM Devils you bastard!

NARRATOR He lunges at Cy and throws him down; he should not have done that though because Futz is quick and kicks his legs out cracking Marjoram's guts hard. The Sheriff fires his pistol a warning shot into the air. Both men relax like drugged sheep.

SLUCK There will be a trial for the man who killed the girl and he'll probably hang! The day will be Monday!

CY I do wish they, folks, wouldn't be mean toward each other.

MARJORAM Mean! He talks about not bein' mean! Whut about Majorie Satz? She's wretched. She's become a bigger tart than she was. She's yapping always about what he did with her and the pig with him, at the same time too he was with her. Crazy evil! Heaven help us working people with Lucifer here in our village!

SLUCK What are you laughing for? It ain't funny when a man's going to die.

CY   I'm not killing. I'm not a judge or lawyer, just a farmer who lives poorly mindin' his own business.

MARJORAM   Well my word! You live here in the town with us. Where's your duty and responsibility?

CY   In my hands. I use them only on my land and in my barn.

SLUCK   I'm gonna tell you that I hate you myself. It isn't right that I as a lawman feel that way. The Constitution says that there should be fairness. But you ruined women, animals and a man's going to die because of you. Futz, I'm gonna do something that my sweet guts don't want, I'm gonna lock you up in the prison because the people might come here, my choppers say yes to your head under their feet, taking good revenge. But I'm gonna lock you up. You'll be safe.

CY   Who'll feed my pig and water my vegetables?

SLUCK   That's not our thought to care about your land and animals. My duty's gonna be lockin' you up in a cell.

MARJORAM   I think he needs death, not just bein' locked up. Futz had done so much harm.

SLUCK   He'll be locked up.

NARRATOR   Futz hurls up his arms as though ready to receive lightning sticks from his friend god, crash them down on the heads of his judgers who want to see him minus, with no thing, no bliss.

CY   I'm a helpless man now, a partridge run after by turkeys!

MARJORAM   Bastud. Lecherous bastud. You'll get yours for spoilin' our lives.

SLUCK   I'll be easier when you pay up your debt to us. You've done a wrong, man.

NARRATOR Futz in the middle walks out with the men, maybe sad jazz could be played now, not too much though.

SCENE 6

NARRATOR Majorie Satz, it's another day, in the field with two men, father and brother. The first is simple. The second is complex.

FATHER I don't know what about anything but Futz should hang though.

BROTHER NED Like Loop, Dad. And the corpses hosswhipped.

NARRATOR Majorie is quiet with her arms hard against her body. She's listening like water.

FATHER My dotter Majie is a good girl. Frisky like her reverent mother.

(The old man slaps MAJORIE's *face)*

MAJORIE Git away from me ya old creep. Nothing was my fault!

BROTHER NED Dad, cut it out! Nothin' is the girl's fault. She's just crazy.

FATHER She is crazy! Should be put away!

MAJORIE Can't be solved this way, nothing can, important thing is that I get revenged.

BROTHER NED Nobody gonna revenge you! Nobody really cares that much.

FATHER I care. Who's gonna marry this tramp if somehow we don't save her honor. Nobody'll git the bitch off my neck if Futz is allowed to get away with what he done. She's gotta get married off or I'll have her around our shack forever.

NARRATOR   The old man is sick by this fact of life.

FATHER   She's just got to be made respectable.

BROTHER NED   Don't Bill Marjoram want to marry her? I get the idea he'd be willing to have the ole slot machine.

MAJORIE   Shet up, ya bastud. Don't call me names.

FATHER   Control that trap! It's a wonder you haven't been killed yet being whut you are. Majorie, you're a poisonous snake. And if I didn't have to live in this village I'd kill you myself. Your daddy or not—I hate you!

NARRATOR   Does Satz mean it? I don't know.

BROTHER NED   The both of you really get me! Spoiling with fight when we got to think of something. Something where we can get Futz. I mean he should be killed! Loop is gonna be killed and Futz should also.

NARRATOR   Brother does not have much feeling when he says this. Does he have a reason for Futz's death? Yes. His sister's honor? No. Well . . .

FATHER   I don't want a ruckus and yet there's gotta be something to happen.

MAJORIE   What he does with animals is dirty.

BROTHER NED   HAHAHaaaahshhhhhushy yeah yeah.

FATHER   Craziest thing I ever heard of.

BROTHER NED   Maybe it's good?

MAJORIE   OOOOOOOOOOOoooooooooohhhh I'm sick!

FATHER   Stop your yellin', tramp. You've muddied yaself with every bloke in the village.

MAJORIE So I have. But it's with men.

FATHER Quit up your braggin'. Slut!

BROTHER NED She sure is.

(BROTHER NED *hunches over with jackal laughter*)

SCENE 7

NARRATOR Oscar Loop is in his cell; his mother is there. She looks like Loop, smaller of course, and wearing old things. It's the day of her boy's death.

MRS. LOOP Oscar, sweet good boy. I didn't do nothing but, but good for you I thought. I told you 'bout God when you were small and polished up your shoes for you when you went to school. I did my best for you, my son.

(*She weeps*)

LOOP Mama, I know you did, Mama, I know you did. But let's make some plans for the wonderful things that I have. (*Takes from his pocket tiny specks of something*) Mama, these are holy bits of something good. They can cause miracles. Make people that are sick well. You know. They can even make a dead thing come alive again.

MRS. LOOP Let me hold some in my hand, maybe it'll cure my arthritis. What are they, my son?

LOOP I call them spice-seed insects, they're alive.

NARRATOR Mother flings her arms to the north and south, letting the insects fly. She squelches a shriek letting something dawn on her. Her son's dream.

MRS. LOOP O son, I'm sorry. But those wonderful seeds are potent, they cured my arthritis so quickly, my hands tingle.

21

LOOP   I knew it would work. I'm so happy. Take care of them I only have a handful. Mother use them wisely, don't give them to no pretty women, only old people and dead things. It's a gift from Siva.

MRS. LOOP   Siva? Who is Siva?

LOOP   A holy thing with lots of arms. She couldn't die with her lots of arms, even if ten brutes tried to do her in. Siva lives and lives.

MRS. LOOP   Siva sounds like she's a good Christian woman. None around here like her. My son hates evil so he justly killed it. Oh son. Oh son, that you should be killed by the villagers is fair though you're my precious blood, it's right. And that you should have killed an evil girl, is right too. No! Nobody—no woman is good, all want one thing from a man, his lust stick!

LOOP   Mother mother mother (*He is weeping*) mother mother mother why couldn't I find you? Why couldn't I ha' been my own father.

MRS. LOOP   Stop it my son (*She is slightly smiling*), that is not a thing to say, but we two are godly and there shall be rest for us both. A son and his mother are godly.

LOOP   A -son-and-his-mother-are-godly. Everything you say is beautiful. Mother, you are like the holy virgin.

MRS. LOOP   That is blasphemy, son. Never say that. Look! Look! Look at me, my boy, watch me. Don't talk—just look at me. See my eyes and nose and lips? Remember my face good so that you see it on the inside of the black hood— Oooo I shouldn't say that but it's all so important to me, that when after—when you are dead they'll come to be with me and grieve. But if they don't? I couldn't stand it, I must feel them all around me, they must be a loving family—all around me, they must feel so sorry for me—because I am a mother with no son.

LOOP   Nothin' nothin' nothin' . . .

MRS. LOOP   Whut?

LOOP   I'm gonna be nothin' (*He rubs his feet on the floor*) nothin'—so? Mother, who's gonna be with you? The folks you like?

MRS. LOOP   Yes. But they've made my life very hard. I need them though. You wouldn't know being a man. You're my son and if you were a minister I couldn't be more proud. I'm saying everything now. I remember when you got tattooed. You said it was manly. I wasn't more proud. (*She opens her bag and lifts out a square package*) I remember when Howard bopped me. Take some fruitcake, son. Your father was jealous of me, you wouldn't dream that I was a good-looking girl to look at me now, but I was and Howard was very jealous of me. You look like me you know, when I was young. And he would say he'd kill me too you know, even before you were born when you was just the fruit of my womb. I'm an old woman now and have not one bit a thing. When I was young I coulda had a lot, cause of my looks. I didn't want anything, just to be happy.

LOOP   Mom—wouldn't it be wonderful if I could make myself invisible? Then I could go away. They couldn't find me. You and me would finally be let alone.

MRS. LOOP   Yes, it would be wonaful (*She's almost in a trance*) Oscar, I forgive you for wanting me to die.

LOOP   Mama, I never meant that really.

MRS. LOOP   I know you didn't. I'm sorry I said that.

LOOP You couldn't die anyway, cause I'd give you the spice insects.

NARRATOR They look at each other as if he's a tot learning to walk. Noise is heard, it's time for Loop to die. When he's dead he won't see any more.

WARDEN Hello Mrs. Loop and Oscar. Mrs. Loop go to my cousin Hattie, she's outside waiting to take you home with her. Oscar you come with me to the middle of town. Right?

LOOP Right, yes yes, right. I'm bad. But I'm gonna keep my feet together when I swing like a soldier.

MRS. LOOP He's gonna look like a minister high on the pulpit above the congregation. I'm going to dress respectably.

SCENE 8

NARRATOR Majorie in a whorey mood, walking with two drunken blokes in the field.

MAJORIE Runnin' bastud. Futz's so scared now.

SUGFORD Aaaaa Harrrr that's good.

BUFORD Pooos. Scared yella. Uuuuuuuuuuuch my stomach hurts.

MAJORIE You have your stomach—Cy's not gonna have his.

SUGFORD Yeah yeah.

BUFORD Gal that was a *creazzy* thing to do with you. I wouldn't ha' done that. I'm bagged.

SUGFORD You bagged? I'm alive.

MAJORIE I'm alive too.

NARRATOR She sits on the grass, the two get down on her sides.

MAJORIE I'm wanting excitement.

SUGFORD Maybe you need to get banged.

BUFORD Me too.

MAJORIE (*Laughing high*) What for?

BUFORD Wha' ya mean, wha' for? For fun.

NARRATOR He picks up a stone and throws it at her. She catches it and starts playing with it, hands cupping it like it's a baby chick.

MAJORIE Let's go nuts us three then clean up somehow.

SCENE 9

NARRATOR A little time later.

MAJORIE Nooooooot enough noooot enough!

SUGFORD We gotta fix it good.

BUFORD Gal, you're a pig.

(*He coughs; then laughs like a madman*)

SUGFORD Yeah, she's a pig. We should chop her up with the other one.

MAJORIE It's too late and I'd be dreary eating. I'm revengeful. Look I know where it is! His sow. Let's kill her. Let's kill his pig!

BUFORD So what for? So? Fat pig wants to kill a pig.

SUGFORD Wou'nt that be like killing yu sister?

MAJORIE Both of you are like mice! Just wanting . . .

BUFORD Git off it.

SUGFORD Girly git off it. You're just askin' for it.

BUFORD You don't know how you could end up.

MAJORIE You don' have to do nothin'. I'll just do it.

SUGFORD Why?

MAJORIE Because I want to.

SUGFORD Buf?

BUFORD Okay.

SCENE 10

NARRATOR Everything is the same.

SUGFORD Who wants it?

MAJORIE She's a dirty dirty thing.

SUGFORD I'm getting away from totty. You don' want to stay here any more, do you?

BUFORD No. Let's just gooooo.

(BUFORD *and* SUGFORD *run off*)

MAJORIE Come back, ya chicken bastards.

NARRATOR   Hell hath no fury like a woman scorned by a man—for a pig.

SCENE 11

NARRATOR   In the prison cell Futz sits very hard. He's blowing out his cheeks and binding his nostrils close to the bone.

CY   Huh -uuh-huh-hh-uuh- Oooooook huuhhhhoooookii- ooook huuuuuh -uuuuhuh-huuuuoook oook Amaaaaan- ddddaaaaa I mis you soooooo, my molly Amaaaaandaaaaa I miiiiiiiissssss youuuuuuuu. Tain't faih my faymale. You were good to me 'nd I was sooo good to you. You ate corn 'nd sleep beside me. We tried to go to church but they wouldn't let us in so I'd read you the Bible at home. My mother was a good Protistin, she'd love you too. Mother, get back in your grave you're stinkin' up the green world!

(WARDEN *comes in*)

WARDEN   Behave yourself. Isn't there any decency in you? Dishonorin' your parent's memory screaming out blasphemies in prison.

CY   Warden, you look like a bad drawing of God.

WARDEN   Futz, I should let the folks take you to them. I should hand you over to them. They'd teach your dead body manners.

CY   You want a war.

WARDEN   I want you legally killed.

CY   You don't have to fear I'll rape your mother she's too old. Or your daughter she's got your bad teeth. Warden, why don't you kill your wife and kids? You know that you're unhappy.

WARDEN I'm a normal man, Futz. It's you that's unhappy. And you've caused treachery.

CY I wasn't near people. They came to me and looked under my trousers all the way up to their dirty hearts. They minded my *own* life. O you're making me be so serious. And I'm only serious with my wife.

WARDEN Your what?

CY (*Screaming*) My wife my wife! And how many tits does your wife have? Mine has twelve.

WARDEN You're ranting, animal.

CY If I was wi' her I'd be grunting.

SCENE 12

NARRATOR It's Satz's place. Dirty. The old man, son and mother are there.

MOTHER Majorie's such a bitch.

FATHER It must ov been the bug's fault when she was born.

MOTHER What d'ye mean?

FATHER I saw a bug on your stomach when she yipped.

MOTHER I was clean when the child was born.

FATHER Clean as a swamp.

MOTHER Swamp! Swamp! No. It was pure water that they had on me.

FATHER Pig piss it was! Why, woman, you're still slying and lying!

MOTHER I'm not gon' to say the story any more.

FATHER Look! Look! The girl is not mine. Not my dotter.

MOTHER She is she is she is!

FATHER She is my dotter? Then why did the bugs sit on your knees crying prayers to heaven?

MOTHER It didna happen!

FATHER It could ov been you with the pig and him—like it was her!

MOTHER I'll call my son. (*Screaming*) Ned! Ned!

(BROTHER NED *comes in*)

FATHER Ned Ned—be dead!

MOTHER Hear him!

FATHER Everythin's made her nervous, Ned. She's mad again.

BROTHER NED Don' be mad. Majorie'll get her honor back again. I'm going to kill Futz.

FATHER Don't do it alone, take someone with you.

BROTHER NED I want to myself.

MOTHER (*Crying*) But wash with pure water, don' leave the blood.

FATHER He could leave the blood. There's no disgrace in fightin' for his sister.

BROTHER NED HAHuuuhahahashus hahhas hohaaahh-Mother, don't fret I won' leave the blood.

MOTHER Before you go, will you have somethin' to eat?

SCENE 13

NARRATOR   He's in the prison with Cy. Ned.

CY   Boy boy boy. You want to kill me. Why?

BROTHER NED   My family.

CY   I've got none just a sow.

BROTHER NED   You make my brains red.

CY   I'll tell you peace.

BROTHER NED (*Screaming*)   Shut up shut up! I don't want to know you!

CY   You don't have to know me—just let me be.

BROTHER NED (*Cold fury*)   Your neck should be boiled.

CY   That's what I don't want to happen to my sow.

BROTHER NED   She'll die too.

CY   Now why Ned why do you want to kill the animal?

BROTHER NED (*Seething*)   You make my brains red!

(*He stabs* CY)

NARRATOR (*Ironical*)   Amanda—there's someone here he needs you. Yes.

Blackout

The String Game

•

THE STRING GAME *was first presented on February 12, 1965, at The Judson Poets' Theater in New York City, with the following cast:*

(In order of appearance)

KESAK	Sandy Cohen
APNAK	David Miller
BONTEMPO	John Coe
KATKA	Jamil Zakkai
NUGAK	Henry Calvert
CECIL	Jerome Raphael
STOREKEEPER	John Quinn
FIRST WOMAN	Cecile Verhaeghe
SECOND WOMAN	Joan Astley

Directed by Lawrence Kornfeld
Music by Al Carmines
Production Stage Manager Anita Ranze
Stage Manager Bob Pasolli
Lighting Technician Kathy Lewis
Technical Advisor Katie Egowa

SCENE 1

Greenland: In a hut, four Eskimos play the string game, and FATHER PAOLO BONTEMPO, *a little priest from Malta, watches.*

KESAK This is a crack in the ice or a man's behind.

APNAK This is a seal or maybe a vulva. (*Grins at* BONTEMPO) Fada, is this a seal or a vulva?

BONTEMPO (*Patiently*) A seal.

KATKA (*Laughing*) Fada has never satisfied himself with a woman and knows nothing of vulvas, of course, but he has seen a lot of seals.

BONTEMPO (*His little hand rubs his shaved pate*) Don't say it that way, so lewdly. (*He picks up a piece of frozen meat and sucks intensely*) Many men in my part of the world never marry, and sometimes for the highest reasons. And if I had, I would not be here with you. Coition isn't everything.

NUGAK We don't think so either; too many children and not enough caribou. My second wife had to strangle two little ones and leave her old mother on the ice because of the famine two years ago. Coition certainly is not everything!

35

APNAK   Listen to "good-by-stink" Nugak talk! The biggest wife trader and enlarged organ ever to get lost in a blizzard—but he follows his nose and always finds a widow. (*Affectionately, with a tinge of envy*) You widow-diddler!

BONTEMPO (*Mildly*)   Stop it, boys. (*Makes a string picture clumsily*) I think I've made an angel or the Lord. What do you think, fellas? Is it an angel or the Lord?

KESAK   A fox trap or a woman's breasts.

APNAK   Your picture isn't very clear, Fada. But it looks sort of like a vulva. But of a very old woman.

BONTEMPO (*Angry*)   No, it's not a woman's breasts or a fox trap, or that word again. Greasy little heathens—sex-minded!

(*He moves toward the far end of the hut and broods*)

KATKA (*Jovially*)   All right, Fada, don't be mad with us. You're like a small child in this country. This is our way of not being bored, talking whatever comes into our heads when we look at the string pictures.

NUGAK   If he says it's an angel or a lily of the field, okay.

APNAK   What is a lily of the field?

KATKA   A flower, a white flower. And an angel is a young girl with hair like the sun.

APNAK (*Pulls out an old movie magazine and finds a picture of a blonde actress or a naked pin-up*)   Here's an angel. (*Kisses the picture*) I like her long eyelashes.

KESAK   Her hair is like the fur of the polar bear.

BONTEMPO (*In good humor again*)   See whatever God wills you to see, my little flock. But let us read together from the Holy Book.

36

(He takes the magazine away, folds it in half and sits on it)

APNAK   Please read to us, Fada. We don't know how.

KESAK   Yes we do! You just want to save your eyesight because of the spirits who might want to take it if they knew you use it for books instead of hunting caribou.

APNAK   That's right, I'm afraid for my eyes. The spirits might become jealous, so you please read, Fada.

BONTEMPO   *(Takes a Bible out of his habit and reads from Leviticus, Chapter eleven, Restrictions on various meats; the Eskimos stare and nod while he reads; all of them except* KATKA *fall asleep)*   Say to the children of Israel: These are the animals which ye are to eat of all the living things of the earth. Whatsoever hath the hoof divided, and cheweth the cud among the beasts, ye shall eat. But whatsoever cheweth indeed the cud, and hath a hoof, but divideth it not, as the camel, and others, that ye shall not eat, but shall reckon it among the unclean. The cherogrillus which cheweth the cud, but divideth not the hoof. And the swine, which, though it divideth the hoof, cheweth not the cud. The flesh of these ye shall not eat, nor shall ye touch their carcasses, because they are unclean to you. These are the things that breed in the waters, and which it is lawful to eat. All that hath fins, all that hath fins, and scales, as well in the sea, as in the rivers, and the pools, ye shall eat. But whatsoever hath not fins and scales, of those things that move and live in the waters, shall be an abomination to you, and detestable: their flesh ye shall not eat, and their carcasses ye shall not touch. All that hath not fins and scales, in the waters, shall be unclean. Do not touch the eagle, and the griffon, and the osprey, and the kite, and the vulture, and the raven, the ostrich, and the owl, and the larus, and the hawk, and the screech owl, and the cormorant, and the ibis, and the swan, and the bittern, and the heron, the houp also, and the bat. Of things that fly, whatsoever goeth upon four feet, shall be an abomination to you. But whatsoever walketh upon four feet but hath the legs behind longer, wherewith it hoppeth on the earth, that ye shall eat. But all the creeping things shall be abominable to you neither shall it be taken for meat. Whatsoever goeth upon the breast on four feet, or hath many feet, or trailing on the earth, ye shall not eat, because it is abominable. Do not defile your souls, nor touch aught thereof, lest ye be unclean. For I am the Lord your God. Be holy because I am holy. Defile not your mouth by any creeping thing, that moveth on the earth. For I am the Lord who brought you out of the land of Egypt, that I might be your God. Ye shall be holy because I am holy. This is the law of beasts and fowls, and of every living creature that moveth in the waters, and creepeth on the earth. That ye may know the differences of the clean, and unclean, and know what ye ought to eat, and what not to eat.

(BONTEMPO *finishes reading and looks at the sleeping men sadly. He lies down and cushions his head with his arms*)

KATKA (*Moves over to* BONTEMPO *and whispers*) Fada, we eat almost anything that we find. There are no olive trees here or orange-colored fruit or yellow-haired women. We are not in a land of milk and honey. We have lots of our own food taboos, like bear liver and heart and human meat. Nobody told you to come here, but we are glad that you're with us.

BONTEMPO Katka, where I come from the people are not made much differently from you. They too have short legs, but they are long on intelligence and love of God and the saints. And they were once given the word too. And now they keep the word very dear. I want your people to do that too. And I want only clean and good things seen in the string pictures. If you keep seeing bad things, you will get a leprosy on your eyes and mouth. Please, no more talk. Let me sleep. The storm will be over soon. God wills it so.

KATKA (*Giving* BONTEMPO *a small kick*) I know you have the picture of a woman under your behind, Fada. A picture of a woman with golden hair the color of a starved rabbit's shit (*Laughing very hard*) and don't think I'm afraid of a disease in your Bible, you smooth-head-like-a-woman's-breast! Listen, I really like you. We all really like you! We don't want you to leave.

BONTEMPO Leave! (*Screaming*) I will never leave, until you are converted and your mothers! Until the awful pleasure of exchanging wives is given up and the still awfuller pleasure of the women nursing their children and other people's children and anybody in general till they are fourteen! Why, the other day I saw Banzak— who's sixteen and a hunter in his own right—nursing at the breast of Nugak's wife!

KATKA But poor Banzak is an orphan and has stomach trouble. He can only take in milk. Whale and seal are too tough for him in his condition, and so he hunts for Nugak, who, of course, feels sorry for him and lets him take his wife's breasts. That is just one kindness for another.

BONTEMPO Katka, you only treat a slave like that. Not a wife! The other way is a union full with the devil's impulses! How do you know Nugak's wife likes it?

KATKA She does. I can tell by the smile on her face. Her eyes and nose become so small. I love a happy woman with a little nose.

BONTEMPO   There you are, Katka! You have slept with Nugak's wife!

KATKA   Yes, and he has slept with mine. It's wonderful to have a change from the same thing day after day. And men become better friends and better partners in hunting.

BONTEMPO   Foulness! And the women get jealous.

KATKA   Why? They don't wear out. They come back happy and as good as ever. But it's up to the husband, one must get his permission. If not, the wife will be beaten.

BONTEMPO   But even the young girls, the unmarried ones, are prey to the men!

KATKA   It's her own business. She has to learn, and she has to find a mate, and they must like sleeping together. That is the right way.

BONTEMPO   It can't be! Lasciviousness is never the way to heaven. And that is where the good go. And goodness knows lasciviousness is bad, evil for God's sake! Katka, wake up.

(*Grabs and hugs and pushes him*)

KATKA   I am awake! (*The other Eskimos wake up*) Here is a man who although white is very ignorant of our ways in the most northern part of the world and this indeed is the most northern part, I mean the priest has said it. We have heard him, at least I have, if you men haven't. I have heard him say that he is with men of another kind in the most northern part of the world and he, who comes from the most southern part of the world, and God I thought I knew the south, but only the south of this part of the world which is the north. That is the south I know. But in this south where there are olive trees and things called fruits, thin skins with plant juice and meat except not from an animal and other lovely things though I've never myself seen a tree, but a priest does not lie about those things and an Eskimo does not lie either and will not either disbelieve a priest and a white man and he is both. But he keeps us curious in these nights of storm and I like him for that.

APNAK (*Rubbing his eyes and scratching*) I like him for the powder that he gave me for my lice. But that doesn't last forever, and so I still scratch. My wife resented me not having lice for a while, so I'm glad to be on the good side of her.

BONTEMPO That's another thing that I don't like about you people, your lice-biting of each other, it's an odd and awful habit. I wish you'd stop it!

APNAK A man may do what he likes with his wife or his lice, Fada.

BONTEMPO (*Screaming*) We are our brother's keeper! We are. We are.

KESAK Who are?

KATKA In his religion, somebody betrayed his brother and brings down the anger of the biggest spirit.

NUGAK The big spirit. Not the biggest, just the big.

BONTEMPO (*Righteously, to* NUGAK) See, you remember very well what I have told you about the Lord!

APNAK But you have told us nothing about the lice and why you don't enjoy biting them.

BONTEMPO Both names begin with *L*. But one is an abomination unto the other. The louse is a little parasite. (*Pauses*) Yea, and we are parasites unto the Lord when we don't listen to him.

KESAK But they're tasty. They're a bit like a sweet codfish.

APNAK   I think more like a very young child's snot.

KATKA   That's the wonder of them, the lice. They are different to each of us. My wife's taste like flowers.

BONTEMPO (*Hurt*)   I had lice and was sent home from the school. My mother rarely washed my hair when I was little, she was a busy woman. There were many of us. Too much to do and wash my hair besides . . . fourteen children . . .

KESAK   I don't see what is so bad about lice. Washing the hair is bad. Although a little urine on it will make it shine.

NUGAK   The Fada has a very good hair around his ears. On top he's very smooth, like a breast of a woman.

APNAK   I like the Fada's eyebrows, so full and long.

BONTEMPO   Do you think I have fine hair and eyebrows? I never considered myself a handsome man, but I myself thought I had excellent hair. I had more of it when I was young. (*Italian music plays and the priest talks; the Eskimos silently play string games and fall asleep*) Blue-black hair like a prince in a fairy tale, or a lovely Portuguese fisher boy, or a beautiful Maltese man. I was small. (*Smiles*) Still am, but I had fun. Not as much as I wanted, but (*Stretches*) blue-black hair. I was not like Franco, so tall, but neither was I like Mario, so short. I was Bontempo the medium-on-the-short-side. I don't want to get snow blind. It happens so often with the whites, though luckily my eyes are dark and give added protection . . . the pigment. Broiled fish with a little olive oil and lemon. How long, Oh Lord! Porgy, I would love some broiled porgy with a bit of oregano. (*Offstage, coughing is heard*) Is that you, Cecil?

CECIL (*Offstage, masterfully*)   Yawohl!

BONTEMPO (*Tired*)   Enter.

(CECIL, *the half-breed, comes in shuffling and suspicious. He glances at the men with contempt. They
watch the following debate with great good humor
and interest, cheering and booing at appropriate mo-
ments*)

CECIL   What is happening here? Fada, what is up?

BONTEMPO   You may be at ease now, Cecil. Nothing's happening. We're waiting for the storm to let up.

CECIL   Waiting for the storm to let up and playing string
games! Look, all around string! It's decadent! (*Pronounces it "deeKAYdent"*)

BONTEMPO   God! If only the other half of you wasn't so
German.

CECIL   That's my better half. It's what makes me realistic!
(*Points his arm viciously at the sleepers*) Not like these
swine! (*Pronounces it "schwine"*)

BONTEMPO   Schvine, you mimicker!

CECIL   (*Enviously*)   Well, you went to college!

BONTEMPO   That's right. I know how to say some words
correctly. So I say sit down and be quiet. Let people sleep.

CECIL   No sleep. I have an excellent idea for all of us. We
will become fishermen. It's neater than meat. We'll import
herring like the Norwegians.

BONTEMPO   You are a dumb-head, yes?

CECIL   Yawohl! No! We must not be on the dole. We should
be in business like everybody else. I may sound like a
European-lover, but . . . well, I am half! But we should
keep up with the rest of the nations and learn money.

BONTEMPO   Learn money? What does that mean? Like
learn war? You can't learn money. You either make it or

43

you don't. And we choose not to make it but to get it, and every now and then if and when we can, the supply is short, catch a seal or a very rare deer. But that's not our fault. I mean, not the Eskimos. They didn't kill too much, just enough to eat. It's the others who killed too much. Your half, the better, and my all.

NUGAK   Cecil, you are a disgrace to the Eskimo race.

CECIL   That's just half of me. You jealous thing.

NUGAK   Every time he comes in I am immediately aware of my killing instinct!

APNAK   Also he messes up the whole mood of these weekends.

KESAK   When I look at him, I feel I know why the caribou have gone. A salmon-cannery starter! (*Contemptuously*) A fish-eater! A tuna-screwer!

KATKA   God! And I really felt I was living like my grandfather and then he comes in. The dull-wit!

BONTEMPO   Yes, he can spoil things, like a rotting onion . . . It's hard to love . . . and always Cecil.

Blackout

44

SCENE 2

In the trading store. All sorts of things are seen—utensils, work tools, clothes, etc. CECIL *is admiring the items.* STORE-KEEPER *is bored.*

STOREKEEPER (*Sarcastically*) Boy, you want things, don't you?

CECIL (*Submissive and ingratiating*) I've got good pots and pans. I eat off fine things. I'm making sure that the quality of things remains fine. So important that things remain fine.

STOREKEEPER Things remain fine, but you don't have a dime without a government check, Eskimo!

(STOREKEEPER *laughs*)

CECIL Just temporarily. A small while.

STOREKEEPER The trouble with you people is that you're not white. That's where the trouble is . . . not being white!

CECIL There's good and bad in all people.

STOREKEEPER And you never have an original thing in your head. Good and bad in all people, hoo!

(*Two sexy white women enter*)

FIRST WOMAN   I want a large frying pan for French ome-
lettes.

SECOND WOMAN   Potholders too.

(CECIL, *smiling and flirting in a supercilious way, goes
over to take a pan off the shelf.* STOREKEEPER *runs
toward him and grabs it away*)

CECIL   I was helping the ladies!

STOREKEEPER   This ain't your store! (*Turns to the women
and smiles*) You know these fools, very childish and eager.
Think everything is theirs.

CECIL   I'm not a fool, I'm half German!

(*The women laugh hysterically*)

FIRST WOMAN   Oh, he's cute. Half German, are you? Oh,
cute.

SECOND WOMAN   Let him give us the potholders and frying
pan, Mister Storekeeper.

STOREKEEPER   (*Gives* CECIL *the items and winks at the
women*)   Here y'are, Mister Eskimo, give the ladies the
items. But first make sure to put them in a paper bag. And
you may take the money and hand it to me. (CECIL *looks
around for paper bags and then bends down to look under
the shelves.* STOREKEEPER *makes grotesque faces for the
women, who stifle their laughter*) The bags are over
there!

CECIL   Where?

STOREKEEPER   Over there, you dumbbell! In front of the
cans of kipper, near the food section.

CECIL (*Sees the bags and smiles; he puts the purchases in a bag and hands it to the women with a grin*) Here, ladies, and if you please, I'll take the money.

STOREKEEPER (*Hissing*) That's right. He'll take the money. That's what the pigs do, take the money!

(*The women look at the* STOREKEEPER *and shush him with their forefingers over their mouths*)

FIRST WOMAN Thank you, cutey-Eskimo-pie.

SECOND WOMAN Thank you, humpty-dumpty.

CECIL Would you like to go to the square dance with me?

STOREKEEPER (*Angrily*) Hand me the money!

CECIL (*Excitedly hands* STOREKEEPER *the money and flashes big grins at the women*) I'd like *both* of you to be with me. Square-dancing is helluva fun.

(*Women start laughing and then control their faces in seriousness*)

FIRST WOMAN But I'm much bigger than you. How would it look?

SECOND WOMAN Why, you're the dearest and cutest dumpty-humpty fat little guy, but no thanks.

(CECIL *looks down at his shape and looks up at them; their mockery dawns on him at last. He exits*)

STOREKEEPER Eskimo! Eskimo!

WOMEN (*Giggling*) Eskimo! Oh, oh, Eskimo!

Blackout

SCENE 3

The hut. KESAK, APNAK, KATKA *and* NUGAK *are playing the string game.*

APNAK   Would you let your daughter marry a Greenlander?

KESAK   I'd let her marry anybody.

KATKA   Anybody who's smart enough to get government checks. Right?

KESAK   Right.

APNAK   I'm making a check with the string . . . Who sees it? Whoever sees it first can have it.

KESAK   Like whoever sees the empty air can have it. Right?

APNAK   Right.

(CECIL *enters arrogantly; the men ignore him*)

CECIL   Still playing string games, fools! No wonder you never get ahead. I read the Finances. I will get ahead. (*Flourishes a copy of* The Wall Street Journal) I will one day wear a hat and cloth coat . . . and, and . . . marry a bleach blonde!

(*The others laugh and snort*)

48

APNAK   How is the Deutsch coming along, Herr Eskimo?

CECIL   I learn very easily, the language is in my blood. Being part German makes it so.

APNAK   Yawohl, of course! (*Deeply*) Mein Herr (*Pronounces it "hairy"*), how is the tuna fish sandwich idea coming along?

CECIL   Not sandwiches. The whole fish. But I can't do it alone, and you schwine won't help me.

(*The others click their tongues and sympathize, tongue-in-cheek*)

APNAK   Oh, too bad. Such terribleness on our behalf.

KESAK   We're such fools. Why, oh why, can't we be full of brains?

KATKA   Like Cecil, who's so free of horse-shit.

CECIL   Horse-scheis!

KATKA   Oh, yes, of course, scheis, the good German word.

NUGAK   Hey, Eskimos! Let's show Cecil that we can do something besides diddle with the strings. Let's show him our little song and dance we've been practicing.

(NUGAK *winks*)

KESAK   Yes, yes. Cecil, you just sit down in this corner and watch like the critic you are.

(KESAK *takes* CECIL *by the shoulders and sits him down*)

APNAK   O.K. Fella Eskimos.

(*They form a line, hands on each other's hips, and strut in soft-shoe style*)

KATKA   First we'll do our Nutrition Song.

49

NUGAK, KESAK and KATKA (*Singing together*)

> I want them warm, young
> and tall. When their
> blood's cold, I
> don't like them.
>
> Milk and meat, that's
> good too.
> What the hell are
> Vegetables! They
> make our dogs piss.

KATKA Now for the other one, boys. The one about my grandmother. (*Singing in high falsetto*)

> My hair's in a knot.
> For going to bed
> with whalers,
> I get some
>   sweetened water.
> I put it on my
>   vulva
> to soothe the pain
>   of gonorrhea
> that the whalers
>   gave me.

And now for one that we know you'll like, Cecil. The name of this song is *Eskimo Says So-Long.* (*Singing*)

> Together
>   I wave my
> arm to the others
>   no word for
>   so-long
>   life on the ice
>   thanks
> is like my wife's large, flat nose.

I'm goin'
to the water like a Norwegian
and marry *their* women
they described them
nice
they can have my
wife—the fat seal!

CECIL   First time you say something right, boys. That's just how I feel. (*Laughing*) My wife, the fat seal.

APNAK   The fat seal kept our grandpaps very warm once.

KESAK (*Bitterly*)   But now we're used to Swedish glug . . . You know we are proved wrong! Glug's better than blubber.

KATKA   Yeah, we're proved wrong. Why eat a waterfowl when you can eat canned ham with tiny green peas?

NUGAK   Eskimos eating ham in the modern world. Shit!

CECIL (*Proudly*)   You know, Eskimos, shit is a Germanic word.

KESAK   You never are going to forget that your mother was jumped and that is how you were created, yeh! (*Sardonically*) Without even the melody of *Lohengrin*.

CECIL   Father was an important trapper. Didn't or couldn't marry Mother, who was in the care of the Catholic nuns.

KESAK   How did your loving father get ahold of your little plump mother? Did he (*Laughing*) snatch her from the arms of the nuns, or did he just beckon with his German finger?

CECIL   He had a deep voice. Probably he said (*Loudly*), "Comme here mein Fraulein and give me a kiss." Romantic people, Germans are.

KATKA (*Laughing*)   And then he jumped her.

CECIL No, no, they achieved coition! Schwine! (KESAK *laughs with the others*) No more talk about my parents! (*Frantic*) Listen, let's go into business making clay pipes.

KESAK What about your *herring* idea?

CECIL It's practical, but . . .

(*He makes a face*)

KESAK Herring is not good enough for you, and besides, they stink.

CECIL They irritate my nasal passages. I never liked herrings, even with sour cream. . . . Clay pipes, my mother's father used to make them. We should make them to sell and maybe get rich.

APNAK I can see it now. Eskimos turning out hundreds of stupid clay pipes.

KESAK And tourists buying them as souvenirs. I doubt if they could use them! Enough of this Cecil-corruption of our innocent splendor. Watch me work the string into erotic pictures. (*Takes string and plays*) What's this?

APNAK Somebody jumping the Queen of Norway.

NUGAK A male genital.

KESAK Wrong, wrong. A seal's vulva!

CECIL There are hardly any more (*Screaming*) seals left, schwine! Think of something for us to do!

(*Eskimos laugh*)

Blackout

SCENE 4

FATHER BONTEMPO's *hut. He is brushing his habit free of dust and humming Italian melodies.*

BONTEMPO What I would love, I mean, what I really miss is a dish of pasta, tomato sauce and olive oil. Anybody looking at my figure knows I'm no glutton. Too thin. But still God gave us taste buds. (*Laughing*) And they should be satisfied once in a while. My southern tongue can't stand the dried fish of the Danes and Eskimos. (*Coughing is heard offstage*) Oh, my German friend, again. Is that you, Cecil?

CECIL (*Very masterfully*) Yawohl!

BONTEMPO Enter. (CECIL *comes in, as suspicious as before*) Relax, relax, there's no one here except the white priest.

CECIL Good to be with one's own kind, even if you are a Maltese man.

BONTEMPO (*Guffawing and silly*) Better than a Maltese cat, aye? Oh, I think that's funny. A Maltese man is better than a Maltese cat.

CECIL I have a proposition, Fada. I have a case of pasta, tomato sauce and olive oil. Anchovies and Genoese sausage.

53

BONTEMPO (*Passionately*) What shall I do? How did you get it? What shall I do?

CECIL Take easy! As you know, I'm half German and therefore a realist. I want to wake up my brothers to the twentieth century. Business. I want us to be in business.

BONTEMPO But they enjoy so much the weekends when I play the fire-and-brimstone priest. The government checks seem to please them, and of course their string games . . .

CECIL (*Shouting*) They are demoralized! They need to have ambition! I have pasta, olive oil, anchovies and Genoese sausage.

BONTEMPO And I need it. What shall I do, Cecil?

CECIL (*Holds up a matchbook and reads from it*) "I'll set you up in a money-making business you can run from home! Everything furnished free. Top men make five to ten dollars an hour. You never invest one cent. Close cover before striking. Send now. Want extra money? Run a money-making business right now from your own home. Start spare time. We will supply all the sales help you need to start earning BIG MONEY first hour. We have helped thousands of men build successful careers by offering: QUALITY PRODUCT. Two hundred and thirty fast-selling dress, sport, work styles for men, women. Far greater selection than any local store. National advertising helps you. HIGH-PROFIT OPPORTUNITY. Earn up to nine hundred and sixty dollars a month extra for just taking eight easy orders a day for these super-comfortable SOKE Shoes. UNLIMITED PROSPECTS. Everybody needs shoes. Friends, relatives, folks where you work. Complete range of sizes fits everyone. High quality means plenty of repeat orders. Rush coupon inside for free business kit! Soke Shoe Manufacturing Company. Fank Falls,

Illinois. Please rush me your free 'Shoe Store in a Sample Case' Big Profit Plan and show me HOW I can make plenty of extra money." And look at the cover, Fada. (*Hands* BONTEMPO *the matchbook*) What do you see?

BONTEMPO   I see a clean-cut fellow with a suit and shirt and tie on.

CECIL   That is how I want to look. I'm tired of denim and fur boots, checkered shirts. I want to be in this shoe business.

BONTEMPO   I don't see how anybody can make five to ten dollars an hour selling shoes here. This is Greenland, not Illinois.

CECIL   It can be done. The Danes wear shoes, and so do the others. They will buy shoes from us. Fada, tell the others, make them eager, convince them. I want them all to send away for the sample kits, I want this to be our business. Help me and you will eat the food of your heart's delight. Fada, I smelled the olive oil . . .

BONTEMPO   You can't imagine how it is when a bit of onion and garlic are simmering in it. Oh, I want it (*Weeps*) so much.

CECIL   The night the Eskimos say "yes" to the shoe business, you and I, Fada, will swallow pasta and olive oil.

BONTEMPO   Let's have it before their "yes," please, please.

CECIL   No. And be a white man, Fada—restrain your passions.

BONTEMPO   I want to, but my mouth likes the food of my native land oh so much.

CECIL   Yawohl! Of course, that's how I feel when I smell apple dumplings. Talk the others into business of shoe selling and you will eat. You will, I know. Yawohl! Yawohl!

(CECIL *exits*)

BONTEMPO Apple dumplings. Like Satan tempting Eve. Can Cecil be the devil tempting me? But a business would be good for the Eskimos, and we might still play our games on weekends. Yes, yes. (*Pirouettes and twines an invisible fork of spaghetti and pops it into his mouth*) Si, si, we all could use new shoes.

Blackout

SCENE 5

BONTEMPO *is with the four Eskimos in their hut.*

NUGAK Listen, I'm not a businessman. I'm a string-game artist.

KESAK There are enough people making money.

APNAK We've got our government checks.

KATKA Shoe salesman. Ugh!

BONTEMPO It would be good for you. Give you a sense of the real Greenland. Danes and other people wear and like shoes. You would have many orders.

NUGAK The pale bastards don't know the pleasure of fresh grass between the toes, soft fur on the outside.

KATKA We don't want orders, Fada. We don't want to do anything—except play the string games.

BONTEMPO Why, what does it do for you? What pleasure do you get from it?

KATKA A piece of cord feels nice around the fingers.

NUGAK Cord is too heavy. You mean string, Katka, many strings teasing each other into pictures. They're alive, like the bodies of the animals our grandparents hunted.

APNAK   Like the women, the men, the dogs and the bears. Everything, even the ice.

KATKA   The strings do come alive around our fingers, Fada. (*Takes the string and makes shapes*) I can make anything I want. I can possess anything I want.

BONTEMPO (*Wistfully*)   The long, thin strands of string do give you pleasure.

APNAK   You're beginning to understand. The strings are soft and satisfying, Fada. They fill us up with peace.

(BONTEMPO *hiccups and shakes his head*)

BONTEMPO   I understand, boys. They sit in your bowels. The strings.

APNAK   What do you mean, sit in our bowels? No, they wake our imaginations up!

KATKA   We create! Anything!

APNAK   Our people liked the string game and played. And we play also.

BONTEMPO   Oh, you know that's not all true. You romantic! Most of the other Eskimos go to Copenhagen and study. Get excellent jobs here in Greenland.

KATKA   Yes, and they create nothing.

BONTEMPO   Enter the shoe business, play the string games, create on weekends. We'll continue things the same old way. Nothing will change. I also want to be filled up with peace!

(BONTEMPO *hiccups again*)

KATKA (*Very suspiciously*)   Fada, are you sure Cecil has nothing to do with your idea of selling shoes?

BONTEMPO   He has nothing to do with it.

KATKA Look at this person on the matchbook cover. (*Holds it up to the others*) Who wants to look like this?

APNAK He looks like the fool who gives us our checks each Monday.

KATKA That's another thing, Fada. No checks if we sell shoes. You can't be gainfully employed and collect the government's money.

APNAK I can't bear the tight suits and ties of the whites. Our necks are too broad, anyway.

KATKA What do you mean, too broad! I've seen loads of walrus-fat whites pushing their necks into those collars.

BONTEMPO The collars feel good. I wear one too. A priest's collar.

APNAK A pious priest. Bontempo the Good.

KATKA He plays with the heathens.

NUGAK Eats the frozen meat with them.

APNAK And he says the collars feel good. We don't believe it, Fada.

NUGAK He tries to persuade us to become shoe salesmen.

KATKA Says anything to make us into shoe salesmen.

BONTEMPO No, not anything. I just think it would be good for your morale. Honest work.

NUGAK (*Excited*) Have you seen our routine, Fada?

APNAK We're entertainers.

KATKA Honest work. Actors and singers, a little dancing.

BONTEMPO Who, you?

APNAK, KATKA and NUGAK Us. We showed our act to Cecil.

BONTEMPO Did he like it?

KATKA I think he liked one song. Let's do a song for the priest. Now listen, Fada, one day if we're really good we'll give up the string games for a while and visit a big city, maybe Copenhagen or Oslo, and try New York City later on.

APNAK, KATKA and NUGAK (*They hold hands on each other's hips and sing*)

> We're Eskimos,
> warm-hearted Joes
> in a cold cold land ho ho ho ho.

KATKA That one's not perfected yet, Fada. (*He sings*)

> Here in this land
> the wind
> blow blow blow.

Does that sound right? Not to me. Oh well. (*He continues to sing*)

> Blow blow
> the wind goes.

APNAK We'll fix it up, but we've got some others.

KATKA Let's do the heavenly one, the priest will like it. It's about an angel. (*He sings*)

> I cry in the morning
> of any weather.
> I feel so bad for my
> brother,
> with generosity
> I need an
> angel's pity,
> my brother my brother
> O mine.

APNAK That's taken after an old Norwegian sea song. (*He sings*)

> He floats like
> a log on his back,
>> all drunken all drunken
>> all drunken;
>> the lovely brother of mine
>>> is sunken is sunken
>>>> is sunken.

BONTEMPO That's good, but depressing.

KATKA Ahh! That makes me feel good. Your pleasure in our songs. Of course, they're different from our own Eskimo folk songs. But in a way they're a development. Depression is often a sign of worthy pleasure.

APNAK A worthy depression.

BONTEMPO Please become shoe salesmen.

KATKA Why?

BONTEMPO So I will lose my depression.

APNAK You want too much, priest of need.

NUGAK I say a priest should and does need a depression.

KESAK Like an enema.

NUGAK Should we become sellers of shoes to please Fada Bontempo?

APNAK Paolo Bontempo. Bontempo preaches shoes.

BONTEMPO Bontempo wants to go home.

KATKA Home to where, priest?

BONTEMPO A little village in Malta. I want the warmth.

KATKA (*Turning to the others*) He wants the warmth.

NUGAK Oh, the warmth. Yes, it is cold here.

APNAK Kesak, guess. Who wants the warmth?

KESAK Little Bontempo.

BONTEMPO Why are you mocking me?

KESAK How can you tell?

BONTEMPO You called me little.

KESAK Is it mockery to know a man's size?

BONTEMPO I want to go home. It's rushing from me, this want. Want to go home, want to go home. It sounds good to me. That piece of a sentence.

APNAK Stop being gloomy.

KESAK I'd be gloomy if I was off the ice for as long as the priest has been on it. Different pot covers, all of us.

NUGAK What a treatment for a man. Take him away from his homeland, make him into a priest. Then the man gets tired of a climate that's cold; wants his own. Tries to make natives into shoe sellers.

APNAK If we become shoe salesmen, Bontempo goes home to Malta. How?

KESAK An arrangement. Bontempo has made an arrangement with Cecil.

KATKA Somethings stinks in Greenland!

APNAK Yes, Cecil figures in this, I'm sure.

KESAK What has Cecil promised you, Fada?

BONTEMPO A lunch.

APNAK A hot lunch?

BONTEMPO Yes. I have chills. (*Shivers*) Hold me.

APNAK What?

KESAK Why not. Come here, Fada. (BONTEMPO *goes to* KESAK *and the Eskimo sits him on his knees*) Better?

BONTEMPO A little. But rub my shoulders; they feel a bit stiff.

KESAK (*He rubs* BONTEMPO's *shoulders*) Did he promise you a Maltese lunch?

BONTEMPO Not just Maltese. You can get it practically anywhere in the southern part of Europe.

KESAK You never did like frozen meat the way we eat it, did you?

BONTEMPO No. My gums feel uncomfortable when the icicles of meat melt against them.

APNAK You know, Fada, that is the best way to eat meat. It lasts much longer in the belly.

NUGAK Don't lecture the priest. People love their own.

BONTEMPO Pasta, olive oil, Genoese sausages. Good, good.

KATKA Yes, we know.

BONTEMPO Become what I want you to become. (*Hugs* KESAK) Say it tonight.

KESAK How can I resist this priest? It means too much to him. And he did play our game on the weekends.

APNAK I am moved. I am really moved.

NUGAK We can take care of Cecil. But we must give to Bontempo our understanding.

BONTEMPO I want understanding. I do.

NUGAK No, that really isn't it. You want a hot lunch.

APNAK   Remember the lore of the North. You understand a man when you feed him.

KATKA   I feel that we can say yes.

APNAK   Can I speak for us all, Eskimos?

ALL   Yes. We are shoe salesmen.

BONTEMPO, (*He gets up from* KESAK's *lap*)   Thanks, thanks. I bless you also.

(BONTEMPO *makes the sign of the cross and exits*)

KATKA   Nugak, you're right. People do love their own. Food. Their own clothes. Sometimes their own women.

KESAK   Ahh, it's the outer world that wants to change the inner one. The foreign influences.

APNAK   I agree. There are outside influences.

NUGAK   Cecil the half-German feels his own outside. It wants to change his inner, which is this country. Greenland *über alles,* thinks Cecil.

APNAK   And now he makes a priest forget his vows.

KATKA   Makes a lure for him of tomatoes and oil.

Blackout

SCENE 6

BONTEMPO's *hut. He is sitting at his little table. It is set for two. He has his head on his arms and he hums along with the record of Italian music. Every now and then he looks up and smiles sweetly, then puts his head on his arms again.* CECIL's *cough is heard outside.*

BONTEMPO Is that you, Cecil?

CECIL Yawohl!

BONTEMPO (*Gaily*) Enter.

> (CECIL *walks in carrying a large case; he puts it down in front of* BONTEMPO)

CECIL Your food.

BONTEMPO I know. (*Opens the case excitedly*) It's here, the oil, pasta, tomato sauce, and the blessed sausages from Genoa. Four beautiful substances.

CECIL Yawohl. It is to your taste. My own is heartier. Forceful people need a forcefuller food.

BONTEMPO Yes. (*Not listening, but fingering the little bottles of oil, etc.*) Of course. I will prepare the delightful food for us. But a short while. My hands will bless the food as they prepare it for us.

65

CECIL You Maltese act so nonsensical about food!

BONTEMPO You mean you have known others?

CECIL Yawohl! I know your type. (BONTEMPO *takes the case and exits.* CECIL *walks authoritatively around the room, poking his nose all over*) This is not a way to keep a hut. Things in it are not neat enough! Organization, there must be organization. Any German can see that! . . . and the priest's sensual love of food. Unhealthy.

(BONTEMPO *enters carrying two bowls of spaghetti. He sets them on the table*)

BONTEMPO Preciousness. My lips, tongue, whole mouth will receive this preciousness. Heaven and earth shall pass away, but my desire shall not pass away.

CECIL Yawohl! Neither shall mine. But for business. A prosperous shoe business.

BONTEMPO Let us eat. (*He takes up a fork and begins to eat*) Eat some warm food.

CECIL (*Laughs*) Your face looks like an old grandmother's waiting for kisses.

BONTEMPO I have a great desire to open my mouth wide. I want you to see the mash. I've made those lovely strings into a mash.

CECIL (*Shrilly*) You will not be disgusting in my presence! You will not insult me!

BONTEMPO It is not an insult for me to open my mouth wide so you may see the mash. (*Opens his mouth wide and points a finger at it*) Look, look, Cecil.

CECIL (*Pushes his own dish away*) I don't want to look in your filthy mouth!

BONTEMPO Pulpy, there's a pulpy mass in my mouth. It

amazes me. How could I have eaten frozen meat before? This mass in my mouth is so warm.

CECIL   Stop it! Shut your mouth! I feel nauseated. It looks like blood in your mouth.

BONTEMPO   Let me open my mouth as I want to, Cecil. It does no harm to you.

CECIL   My father taught us to keep our mouths closed when we chewed! He was a good man! Bontempo, if you open your mouth again, I will discipline you with a slap!

BONTEMPO   (*Opens his mouth wider*) Cecil, look, *look!* (CECIL *leans over and slaps* BONTEMPO *sharply on the face.* BONTEMPO *begins to cough and sputter. He falls off his seat and gasps while* CECIL *watches in amazement*) O Lord, I am wicked and slothful. I am an hungred, and ye gave me warm . . .

(BONTEMPO *dies*)

CECIL   (*Panicky*)   I did not want him to choke. It was not my fault!

(CECIL *exits*)

Blackout

SCENE 7

The four Eskimos are playing their string games when
CECIL *bursts in.*

CECIL   It was not my fault! I did not despise him!

(The four look at him with interest)

KESAK   Something was not Cecil's fault!

APNAK   Tell us what's not your fault, Cecil.

CECIL   The priest choked to death on a hot lunch.

NUGAK   *(Turns to the others and they all sigh)*   O he is home, he is home.

CECIL   It's not my fault.

NUGAK   We cannot go into business with you now. We cannot be shoe salesmen.

KESAK   I feel very sad. I loved Bontempo. No, Cecil, none of us can sell shoes.

CECIL   Because I was with the priest when he died?

KATKA   Yes. Death is too close to you now. You cannot be a lucky businessman.

APNAK   Though we know really it wasn't your fault. Still it would be unlucky to go into a business.

KESAK Especially at this time. Maybe next year.

CECIL Next year, then. The shoes.

APNAK Maybe Kesak's right. Next year.

KATKA Bontempo has the climate he wanted.

KESAK The warmth. But not hell. He wasn't a bad man. I'm sure he's not in hell.

NUGAK Would he be considered a glutton according to his religion?

APNAK Who knows? But he looked for peace. And there can't be a sin in that.

CECIL So you say next year, about the shoe business?

APNAK Still thinking about industry, aren't you?

CECIL Well, we must be like other nations. "The hand of the diligent shall bear rule."

KATKA We four simples do not wish to rule.

NUGAK You are a seducer, Cecil. You seduced the good Fada with the food.

APNAK You're a pig with a pig's snout.

KESAK You spoke deceitfully to the Fada and to us. We should leave you on the ice!

CECIL It was not my fault that he died on food! He thought the shoe business would be good for us too!

KESAK No, he really didn't care about money. He was a pious man. Though perhaps he loved a warm meal just a little too much.

KATKA Who knows what is what? Food, piety, gluttony.

KESAK No gluttony. Fada just wanted some warmth.

CECIL   He was a glutton. He opened his mouth up so that I could see the chewed-up stuff!

NUGAK   How dare you call Bontempo a glutton! Cecil, you should wash your own mouth out with snow.

KESAK   Cecil, get out of our sights! (*Pause. Nothing happens*) Raus!

CECIL   Yawohl!

>   (CECIL *clicks his heels, does an about-face and exits*)

NUGAK   I hate to be sorrowful. Let's have some glug and cheer up . . . (*Gets bottles and passes them around*) I wish my grief would dry up.

KESAK   Yes, we wish it too.

APNAK   Let's play a string game. I'll make us something that will make us happy. (*Works the string*) What's this?

KATKA   Two walruses.

NUGAK   A small boy peeing.

KESAK   A hunter or a woman fishing by an ice hole.

APNAK (*Singing*)

>   Ayorema . . . How wonderful
>   for us all that God was born
>   to make us friends of his
>   in a land of happiness . . .
>   bring your skins
>   and your fat flesh
>   to my poor house.

This is a vulva of a seal.

>   (*The Eskimos laugh*)
>
>   *Blackout*

Beclch

BECLCH *was first presented on December 20, 1966, by The Southwark Theatre Company at The Theatre of The Living Arts in Philadelphia, with the following cast:*

(In order of appearance)

BECLCH (pronounced Beklek)	Sharon Gans
YAGO	Jerome Dempsey
THIN MAN	Ronald Roston
SLEEPING MAN	Arthur Hall
OLD WOMAN	Miriam Phillips
BOY	Adam Gopnik
PREACHER WOMAN	Lois Smith
MANK	George Bartenieff
NUALA (pronounced Noola)	Crystal Field
SINGERS	Tom Brannum
	Merwin Goldsmith
ACCOMPANIST	Deborah Sussel
JOSE (pronounced Hosee)	James John Little
BARTENDER	Merwin Goldsmith
CUSTOMER	Sam Schacht
FIGHTING COCKS	Sonny Streater
	David Swenson
FIGHT CROWD	Ed Bernard
	Arthur Hall
	Richard Moten
	H. Latta Pinkerton

73

BELL DANCERS	Arthur Hall
	Richard Moten
HERMES	Kevin Coleman
WORM WOMEN	Vangie Brown
	Carol Butcher
	Karen Steptoe
NATIVE WOMAN	Marilyn Coleman
NATIVE SERVANT	Karen Steptoe
THE THRONE, THE SICK; PILE OF	Afro-American
CARCASSES	Dance Ensemble
INSTRUMENTALISTS	John Arnez Blaine
	George Cannon
	Robert Crowder

Directed by André Gregory
Sets by John Conklin
Costumes by Eugene Lee
Lighting and graphics by Richard Nelson
Music by Teiji Ito
Masks and special properties by Ralph Lee
Dances by the Afro-American Dance Ensemble, under the
direction of Arthur Hall
Environment Consultant Carolee Schneemann

A NOTE ON THE COSTUMES

The native men and women wear bright-colored fabrics draped around the waist. Any exposed parts of the body are garbed in a black body-stocking; the nipples of the women's breasts are drawn or painted in fantastic colors. Hermes is "nude"; he wears an entire black body-stocking and a little red penis. The cock-fighters wear green body-stockings and masks. Beclch, until the time she becomes Queen, wears a darkish red, purple, green and rust robe which is dirty; when she is Queen, she wears a brilliant purple robe with zig-zags of bright red and yellow; her feet are always bare. Yago wears dark pants and a dark shirt. When he becomes King, he wears a dark-colored robe and a yellow skullcap; his decoration is his obscenely swollen leg, fantastic and grotesque. His fingernails are long and red. Mank and Nuala wear bright-colored robes. Jose is blond, boyish, but very male. He is bare to the waist and wears very tight, low-hipped, light-blue bell-bottom pants. He wears a leather wrist guard and a beautifully ornate motorcycle belt. He walks like a cat. The others are dressed normally.

". . . Schism in the souls of members of a disintegrating society displays itself in a variety of shapes because it arises in every one of the various ways of behaviour, feeling and life which we have found to be characteristic of the action of human beings who play their part in the genesis and growths of civilizations. In the disintegration phase each of these single lines of action is apt to split into a pair of mutually antithetical and antipathetic variations or substitutes, in which the response to a challenge is polarized into two alternatives—one passive and the other active, but neither of them creative. A choice between the active and the passive option is the only freedom that is left to a soul which has lost the opportunity (though not, of course, the capacity) for creative action through being cast for a part in the tragedy of social disintegration. As the process of disintegration works itself out, the alternative choices tend to become more rigid in their limitations, more extreme in their divergence and more momentous in their consequences. That is to say, the spiritual experience of schism in the soul is a dynamic movement, not a static situation. . . ."

—Arnold Toynbee

ACT ONE

●

SCENE 1

A field in Africa. A hut is in the background. Stage right, there is a very large sack of bones; some of the bones are spilling out. A few firecrackers are lying about. BECLCH sits stage center, cross-legged. YAGO rubs her neck.

BECLCH (*Sighs*) Your fingers are good . . . you rub well. (*Laughs*) They feel like magnets . . . your fingers.

YAGO Don't talk.

BECLCH (*Playful*) I want to talk. I like to talk. If you were always around me . . . twenty-four hours . . . a whole day . . . I would serve you meat . . . and you would have one iron fork.

YAGO (*Laughs*) That's good, one iron fork, one eating tool.

BECLCH (*Smiles*) One eating tool. You know, in an ancient time, in Egypt, a cat could eat from the plate of its master, but a slave couldn't—he would be laid out *flat* for it.

YAGO (*With slight sarcasm*) You know so much. You have a good sense of humor . . . too.

BECLCH That is a value. (*She enunciates "value," throws her head back, looks at YAGO and smiles*) Put a V on my stomach.

77

YAGO (*He draws a V with his forefinger and shouts*)   Be put there!

BECLCH (*Irritably*)   Your voice is hollow. Say it again—lighter, marvelous.

YAGO (*Tonelessly*)   Lighter, marvelous.

BECLCH (*Angrily*)   No, no! Say, "Be put there"!

YAGO (*Loudly*)   Be put there!

BECLCH (*Contemptuously*)   You speak language hollowly! Your tongue must be diseased—maybe all you're good for is a freak show! (*Pause*) Your hands are incredibly hot—take them away!

YAGO (*Angrily*)   You are not understanding! You'll be forbidden to stay here!

BECLCH (*Mimicking him*)   I am not understanding! I'll be forbidden to stay here! I'll rule here! (*Hits him*) Take that, you sardine! Take that from a sea urchin!

YAGO (*He grabs her wrist*)   Take it easy . . . sea urchin.

BECLCH (*Pulling away*)   I *am* understanding—you cannot say that you'll forbid me to stay here! This—all this is my place!

YAGO (*Tonelessly*)   Yes, sea urchin, this is your place. (*Rubs his fingers on his mouth. Pause*) You have made my mouth bleed.

BECLCH (*Slight sarcasm*)   I'll get a linen cloth for your mouth.

YAGO   I will get the cloth.

(YAGO *exits*)

BECLCH (*Standing with her legs spread wide and her arms crossed*)   I have never oppressed anything or anybody—

I've only defended—tender things, I've defended—things which kick with their hind legs. (YAGO *returns. He dabs a cloth to his mouth*) Is your mouth fixed now?

YAGO (*Brooding*)   It is fixed.

BECLCH (*Preachy*)   There is not one among us who is without perversion.

YAGO (*Tolerant*)   That is for sure.

BECLCH   And I can never be dastardly or foul-mouthed.

YAGO   Mischievous—you are mischievous. One day you'll split like a broiled fish because of your mischief.

BECLCH (*Angrily*)   You smell! Get dumb! (*Shouting*) Monkey! Red-nailed monkey!

YAGO (*Becomes furious, catches his breath and has a fit of coughing*)   You . . . are . . . infamous!

BECLCH (*Contemptuously*)   You pervert! You coughing pervert! (*Exasperated*) You make me suffer! You make me suffer!

YAGO   I've never bothered you. We are just mammals, mammals, remember.

BECLCH (*Disgusted*)   Stop your philosophy! Your mucus-spasms! Your virtue! Mammals, mammals—I'll show you. (THIN MAN, OLD WOMAN, PREACHER WOMAN *and* BOY *enter. One of the women chews on a bone. The* THIN MAN *carries a large slab of wood.* BECLCH *goes to him*) What the hell are you going to be—a sandwich? (*Laughs*) Well, I hope the Lord blesses you real good! (*Looking him up and down. Pause*) O you are a beautiful man. O but so thin! Bet your thighs are bluish-white. (*Laughs*) O, and I bet your hands are patriarchal. What's the matter, cat got your tongue? Is a prayer lodged in your throat? Can you at least fart!

YAGO (*To* BECLCH, *in a sing-song voice*) Vul-gar. You are a sw-ine.

BECLCH (*Turning to* YAGO, *angrily*) Swat the African flies from your own mouth!

YAGO You are talking barbarously.

BECLCH Barbarously! That's a good one! (*To* THIN MAN) Okay—get the bones! (*He is confused and just stands.* BECLCH *shouts*) Get the bones! (BECLCH *points to the sack of bones*) Get the bones! (THIN MAN *drags the sack of bones to the center.* BECLCH *looks at them and shakes her head. Sinisterly*) That is a *fearsome* pile! Now get . . . your mother.

THIN MAN (*Helplessly*) My mother isn't . . .

BECLCH (*Screaming*) Get her! Get her! (THIN MAN *goes to* OLD WOMAN *and takes her hand, bringing her to* BECLCH. BECLCH *speaks coarsely*) She walks like she's stuffed up with rocks! Christ—how old are you, a hundred?

OLD WOMAN (*Trembling*) Yes, I'm a hundred.

BECLCH (*Sinisterly*) Want to be in the middle of bright lights?

YAGO (*Contemptuously*) Crude.

BECLCH (*To the* OLD WOMAN) Okay, get on top of those rocks.

OLD WOMAN Those are not rocks—they are bones.

BECLCH (*Leering*) Okay, get on top of those bones. Dem bones!

(OLD WOMAN *looks at* THIN MAN)

THIN MAN (*Shrilly*) My hands are tied!

Beclch

BECLCH (*Cynical*) His hands are tied. (OLD WOMAN *goes to the sack of bones and starts crawling around in them.* BECLCH *shrieks to her*) Are you itching? Are you itching now? (*Screaming*) Because I am! You are going to be skinned! Do you know that! You are going to be skinned! (*Points to the* THIN MAN) You are the barbarous mother of him! You are shrewd when it comes to his food and socks—but no longer will you sap the ordinary days from him! (*The* OLD WOMAN *is trying to cover herself up with the bones, attempting to hide.* BECLCH *and everybody is surprised at this. Pause*) Come out! If you come out you will suffer no bad consequence! Come out—don't be timid! You astonish us!

YAGO (*Facetious*) A very inventive old lady. (*To the* THIN MAN) I hope Beclch doesn't beat her up.

> (*He goes off to the side, sits on his haunches and watches*)

THIN MAN (*Shrill*) Beating up a quinquagenarian! It's hideous—I am stumped by all cruelty—I cannot watch! (*He starts to leave, then shrieks*) Mother, stay where you are! Don't come out—you'll be beaten!

OLD WOMAN (*Gasping and weak-voiced*) You all disgust me—but I forgive you . . . I forgive you . . . all this dumbfounds me . . . I grow weak.

BECLCH (*Sardonic*) Her flesh will nourish the earth. She was a good soul.

> (BECLCH *looks satisfied. Pause. She walks to where the firecrackers are lying, picks one up and goes to the* BOY *and the* PREACHER WOMAN, *who is chewing on a bone. The* BOY *and the* PREACHER WOMAN *are nervous*)

81

BOY (*Innocent, high-voiced*) I love my mother—she's a good soul!

BECLCH (*Patiently*) Your mother's a burdensome woman. She's an honest penny, though. That much can be said. (*Smiling*) Ask her if she has reached the marrow of the lamb bone yet—if she has—see if she gives you any of it. (*To* PREACHER WOMAN) Old thingumabob, are you going to give some of the marrow to the boy?

PREACHER WOMAN I never have and I never will!

BECLCH (*Cynical*) An honest penny. (*To* BOY) Meat cooked the African way is very tricky, it gives gas. You're better off not eating any of it. (*Pause*) You look like you have poor resistance to things—bad influences.

PREACHER WOMAN (*Arrogantly*) He gets all of my influences, but he's not gettin' any of this marrow! (*Laughs*) He gets stained by me, stink from me, and little bits of friendship. (*Screaming*) He and I are the same! But none of this marrow! No sir! None of this marrow!

BECLCH (*Contemptuously*) Batty foul old bitch. (*To* BOY) Don't believe her—you and she are not the same. Your bones are very different.

PREACHER WOMAN (*Shrill*) He's the same as me! He imitates me! (*Pulls a mask out of her bag*) Here's a king's mask, son. Put it on. (BOY *puts the mask on. Pause.* PREACHER WOMAN *asks eagerly*) Remember when we walked on the beach looking for shells? You made trumping noises! This mask, you wore it on the beach that day, too, muffled your mouth and you made trumping noises for speech. (*Pause. Slyly*) I manipulate you, boy!

(PREACHER WOMAN *laughs*)

BECLCH (*Hands the* BOY *a firecracker*) Hurl this at her, boy —that'll keep her out of your hair!

PREACHER WOMAN (*Grabs the firecracker from* BOY) I'll turn you into *the fat of milk,* boy! I'll ruin your health if you disrespect me!

BECLCH (*Screaming*) Hit her on the snout! She's not head of the world—hit her on the snout!

PREACHER WOMAN (*Frantic*) I'll choke the boy—I'll choke my son—if you don't stop!

BECLCH (*Cynical*) Your mother . . . has a lot of passion in her belly, boy. Don't touch her.

BOY (*High-voiced*) I love my mother—she's a good soul!

BECLCH Has she told you, women are naturally better?

BOY O yes! (*Proud*) She is a *great mother!*

PREACHER WOMAN (*Smugly*) See! He loves me . . . like a little sheep loves the good shepherd. I'm never really harsh with the boy—so long as he's good!

(*She pulls out a hunk of hair from the* BOY's *head*)

BECLCH Why did you do that? Pull out his hair!

PREACHER WOMAN Ducks lose feathers—snakes their skins! This boy, some of his hair.

(*She laughs*)

BOY (*Innocently*) It does not hurt—I love my mother!

BECLCH (*Bitter*) She's a worm, boy.

PREACHER WOMAN (*Angrily*) Call me a worm! A worm!

BECLCH (*Coldly*) Yes, a worm!

BOY My mother's a good soul—I don't care if she pulls out my hair!

PREACHER WOMAN (*To* BOY) You feel cooler—say it—your skull's a bit cooler—better to *think* with a cool skull!

(*To* BECLCH) You know, sometimes this boy burns up—
hot as a hoot owl!

BOY (*Laughing*)   I'm my mother's hoot owl! (*Embraces*
PREACHER WOMAN) You are a good soul!

BECLCH (*Gently*)   She hurts you, boy. Don't you know that?

PREACHER WOMAN (*Proudly*)   I'm a hero to him! I instruct
him! I'm the sunshine on his back! (*Pause*) You know,
he was born with a *perpetually aching back*—and I shone
on him like sunshine! I warmed him up! (*To* BOY) Boy,
do you ache?

BOY   O no, Mother! Show Beclch, Mother! Show her that
you are like sunshine! (*Proudly*) Show her what a
preacher you are!

BECLCH (*Confused*)   Preacher, sunshine? You mix me up!

PREACHER WOMAN   We didn't mix you up, your own low-
mindedness did that! (*Pause, slyly*) Care to hear me
preach, bitch! It'll do you good. Your sins are flashing
like firecrackers, you know. Firecrackers! You wanted my
boy to throw a firecracker at me! Your *sins* are flashing!

BECLCH (*Facetious*)   All right, goat! Preach.

PREACHER WOMAN   I need a stimulus . . . something proper
for my mood. (*Pause*) uh, uuuuuuuuuuuuu. (MANK *and*
NUALA *enter. The* PREACHER WOMAN *sees them and gestures to them*) Ooooo, come here, you two. Perfect! Girl,
frighten up a bit—mister, heighten yourself up with
pride! (*Pause*) O what a fat sexy mouth you have, girl.
Mister, put your hands on the girl's breasts. (MANK *puts
his hands on* NUALA; *the* PREACHER WOMAN *smiles, then
looks sternly at them*) No wickedness in your eyes—
righteousness—that's what I want to see—righteousness!
(*Turns to* BECLCH) Beclch, this is for you, and you listen
good! (*Pause. She speaks with quick, rhythmical preach-*

ing) Yes God put a body on come on back and rise while I'm in the *flaesh* like you yes and it must be that's right must be written of the law Moses must be fulfilled music and David was a fool and slow of heart and God wanted things done and they fell down and he rose like a proverb so nobody plays music in Amos' house hypocrites don't want to sing they make not no song yes yes your image is yourself God didn't what? Want them to sing yes and they eat up the calf in the stall that was written in the law of Moses uhhuh yes that's right done preached and practiced go this way not the other way the other way is hell get me clear now I'm backed up by the true church began at Jerusalem. (NUALA *quickly pushes herself away from* MANK's *hold. The* PREACHER WOMAN *sees this and looks at* MANK) Hold her! (MANK *gets hold of* NUALA's *breasts;* NUALA *giggles softly*) Nowhere cun a woman be a deacon and you cannot marry while the other spouse lives becuz omission of sins in the name of Jesus Christ not father son or Holy Ghost in the name of Jesus Christ beginning in Jerusalem for all nations uhhuh you're my witnesses I'm gonna send something on you I'm gonna send the Holy Ghost on you and Judea and Samaria everything's gonna sprung up you hear that? You gotta follow the Apostles to hitting of the end of the earth don't go away from Jerusalem obey nobodies gonna have an excuse who? Nobody nobody will get away. (*Pause*) Amen. (*To* BECLCH) That do you any good, huh?

BECLCH (*Angrily*)   No—no good!

MANK (*Facetious*)   O it did me good—it made me tremble!

PREACHER WOMAN (*Pompously*)   You sure it wasn't because your hands were on her?

MANK (*Slyly*)   Maybe yes . . . maybe no.

BECLCH (*To* PREACHER WOMAN, *malevolently*)   You are sly

. . . why did you want these two standing before you . . .
while you *preached!*

PREACHER WOMAN (*Shaking her finger*) A lesson for my
boy, another one of my instructions! Human bodies—
I wanted him to see and be aware of two human bodies
—this angular man and the *fatty* woman—and how the
very arteries inside their skin were singing to each other
—while I spoke about God—these two—wanted to copu-
late (*Pause*) while vaguely listening to my humming
. . . and it was a hum to them . . . as long as their bodies
. . . were so close! Pores smelling pores, his, hers, all a
hum to them—my talk of God—their thought was only to
breed—like hound dogs!

NUALA (*Tremulous*) O it was not so!

PREACHER WOMAN (*Scornful*) A milkmaid's face on the
body of a hound dog! (*Pause; she leans toward* NUALA)
You know, girl—in thirty years your flesh will be *stringy!*
(NUALA *laughs*) And your giggles will be like the neigh of
a horse—your eyes will pop out like a tropical fish!
(*Pause, to* BOY) Son, touch the girl! (*The* BOY *touches*
NUALA's *waist;* MANK *looks cynical*) Feel her arms, son.
Her face—her legs—her feet!

MANK (*Facetious*) What is . . . all this feeling for?

NUALA (*Looks into the* BOY's *face and embraces him*) The
boy's eyes are pretty!

PREACHER WOMAN (*Nodding*) Pretty . . . yes . . . he has
pretty eyes and I think that he thinks you have pretty
eyes, too.

BECLCH (*Coldly*) What are you trying to prove—you
huckster!

PREACHER WOMAN (*Matter-of-factly*) I'm proving to my

son—that life is sometimes rosy on this earth—that sometimes the tsetse fly is driven away.

BOY (*Holding tightly on to* NUALA) O my heart is melting in me, Mother!

PREACHER WOMAN (*Gently*) Yes, good.

BOY O Mother, I love the lady—her eyes make my heart melt!

MANK (*Lewdly*) She's too *big* for you, boy.

PREACHER WOMAN (*Furious*) Shut up, you weird tramp! You leech!

BOY O Mother, I can't stand it any more! I want this beautiful lady!

PREACHER WOMAN (*Patiently*) Yes—but remember—things are not what they seem—in thirty years, maybe less, she'll smell like a greasy cheese!

BECLCH (*Disgusted*) O no! Your lesson to your son is a hangnail to us—we don't need it.

PREACHER WOMAN (*Angrily*) You don't need it! What do you need? Somebody killed!

BECLCH (*Boiling*) Old thingumabob—you are nerve-racking!

MANK (*Goadingly to* BECLCH) She ought to be stuck in a swamp—ridiculing us!

NUALA (*Picking up* MANK's *tone*) Hurting all our feelings! Telling the boy that I smell like a greasy cheese! Filling the boy up with—bad knowledge!

BOY (*Quickly breaks from* NUALA's *embrace, dashes to the* PREACHER WOMAN *and throws his arms around her*) I love my mother—she's a good soul!

(BECLCH *picks up a rock and lunges at the* BOY, *smashing it at his back. He falls*)

PREACHER WOMAN (*Bending over the* BOY, *who is dying*) O his back! His poor back! His poor poor back! He's not good for marrying now—what woman would have acquaintance with him now—now that he's dying!

(PREACHER WOMAN *sobs*)

BECLCH (*Disgusted*) O he's not dying!

PREACHER WOMAN (*Screaming*) He's beginning to shrink in death!

MANK I don't see him shrinking!

NUALA Is he shrinking?

BECLCH (*Disgusted*) No, he's not shrinking.

PREACHER WOMAN (*Wailing*) His poor blood—his poor sperm!

NUALA Where's his sperm—I don't see any sperm.

MANK O, o, there's no sperm. She's insane!

BECLCH (*To sobbing* PREACHER WOMAN) Stop your bupadups, crone! Insane crone!

PREACHER WOMAN (*Touching* BOY) He was as lovely as a butter-and-eggs flower—my lamb!

BECLCH (*Snarling*) Always food on your mind!

MANK Vicious man-eater!

NUALA Disgraceful woman!

PREACHER WOMAN (*Looking at the body of the* BOY) O my darling! O my darling! I'm full of doubt—they've wiped away my eyes, my wisdom—I'm blind!

BECLCH (*Savagely*)   Get dumb also!

NUALA (*Giggling*)   Dumb dumb bitch dumb dumb bitch!

PREACHER WOMAN (*Holding the* BOY's *body in her arms, looking into his face*)   Did I brag too much? Why? The lizards, seeds of violets, you saw—blame who? Blame who? Who shall I blame? One half of a minute and you're dead. What a terrible hue on your face! I've had no victory! O my son!

BECLCH (*Hunching herself over the* PREACHER WOMAN *and* BOY)   Admit that the boy cramped your life—goat!

MANK (*Cupping his hands to his mouth and screaming*)   To hell with you, toothless!

NUALA   Let her rock him in her arms!

PREACHER WOMAN (*Crying*)   Murderers! Murderers!

NUALA (*Going to her and spitting*)   You blowzy pig—I spit on you.

BECLCH (*Putting her mouth to the* PREACHER WOMAN's *ear*)   Plumpk him into a grave!

MANK   There's no grave.

NUALA (*Excited*)   Let her dig one! Let her claw up the sludge with her fingers!

PREACHER WOMAN (*Pleading*)   I'm tired, tired, old . . . O my son, my son!

BECLCH (*Coldly*)   Prepare a grave and plumpk him into it!

NUALA (*Jumping and excited*)   The boy will enrich the earth! Think of that! He will enrich the earth!

BECLCH (*Putting a hand on the* PREACHER WOMAN's *neck and pressing down*) Dig! Dig (*To* NUALA) Nuala, giggle!

Let her hear your lovely giggle! You, Mank! Look reverent!

(BECLCH *smiles*)

MANK (*Facetious*) I do not feel reverent . . . it would be fake.

BECLCH Then look *fakely* reverent! (*To* PREACHER WOMAN) Dig! Dig!

(*The* PREACHER WOMAN *starts feebly to dig*)

MANK (*Appreciative*) This is like Christ's passion!

NUALA (*Calling to* PREACHER WOMAN) The boy's toes are dirty! (*To* BECLCH) Make her clean his toes!

BECLCH Excellent! (*To* PREACHER WOMAN) Clean his toes! (*The* PREACHER WOMAN *picks up the edge of her dress and begins to wipe the* BOY's *toes.* BECLCH *pushes the* PREACHER WOMAN's *head into the feet of the* BOY) With your . . . lips . . . and tongue . . . your lips . . . and tongue. (*The* PREACHER WOMAN *cradles the feet of the* BOY, *licking and kissing his feet and crying.* BECLCH *grabs her by the hair, forcing her head back*) Your boy has long legs—tell his long legs your little bit of woe! (BECLCH *nods a yes*) That's right . . . tell his long legs . . . how heartless we are.

(BECLCH *lets go of the* PREACHER WOMAN's *head; the* PREACHER WOMAN *drops her head on the* BOY's *knees, sobbing*)

MANK (*Screaming*) Make her put spikenard on him!

BECLCH Excellent! Spikenard on him.

NUALA Ahhhhh, they'll both be so fragrant-smelling—so sweetly pungent! (*She dashes off and comes back*) Here is spikenard!

90

(*She throws it to* PREACHER WOMAN)

PREACHER WOMAN (*Rubbing the body*) My lambikin—my
love! My lambikin—my love . . .

MANK (*Appreciative*) Her mother's lovingness . . . beautiful . . . beautiful!

NUALA (*Chanting*) Domina domina domina domina
domina!

(BECLCH *and* MANK *pick up the chant*)

MANK (*Reflectively*) Toothless, bony elbows, flimsy breasts
. . . but ahh her lovingness!

NUALA I'm jealous. I want to rub him too—the very same
way she does. (*She goes to the body and strokes it, looks
into the* BOY's *face and pauses*) O, a bit of blood comes
out of his eyelids! (*She bends her face down and kisses
the eyes, sexily*) O . . . this bit of blood is better than
butter!

(NUALA *laughs*)

MANK I think I'm smelling it, blood—the smell's making
me nauseous.

BECLCH (*Excited*) The smell's making me tremble! I have
the nose of a wolf, now.

(BECLCH *laughs*)

PREACHER WOMAN The snout of a wolf—you killed my son!

MANK (*To* PREACHER WOMAN) You watch out—you watch
our feelings . . .

BECLCH (*Laughing*) Shut up, Mank! (*Moves closer to*
PREACHER WOMAN) I am the wolf that killed the kid—
you gall me—no . . . no . . . more than the wolf—I
am more than the wolf . . . I am the slaughterer. (*She*

pushes the PREACHER WOMAN's *face into the* BOY's *groin*)
Smell it up—that's what you want! Yes!

NUALA (*Giggles*) O his eyelids fluttered! I think I saw his
eyelids flutter! (*Puzzled*) But he's dead!

MANK Reflexes. The dead nerves are still sensitive . . .

NUALA (*Wistful*) What eyelids, so tender, pretty! I want to
look under the lids—to see if fire is still there.

MANK (*Laughing*) Fire, where?

NUALA In his eyes. (*She lifts up the* BOY's *eyelids*) O it's
gone—fire's gone—smashed mosquitoes—his eyes look
like smashed mosquitoes.

BECLCH (*To* PREACHER WOMAN) Doesn't that break your
heart, you old bladder! Your boy's eyes look like smashed
mosquitoes. Why don't you poke around him? Weep! Be
maternal.

MANK Old bladder—be maternal (*Thrilling*) Ooooo lovely!
Grieve for your son—your little rabbit!

BECLCH (*Hotly*) She puts such—urges in me! (*Screaming*) O weep around him—be excessive! Weep, weep!
Poke around him—weep—like there is famine in the land!

(*The* PREACHER WOMAN *is sobbing and gasping*)

MANK (*Calling to* PREACHER WOMAN) Stroke—gently
stroke his windpipe! Oooooo, that's so comforting—the
windpipe being gently stroked!

BECLCH (*Gives the* PREACHER WOMAN *a rabbit punch*)
Don't you be slow! You . . . *stroke* . . . like Mank says!

PREACHER WOMAN (*Falling over* BOY's *body*) My heart is
robbed! O my beautiful son.

BECLCH (*Furious*) You . . . drop . . . of . . . shit. You
pulled *hair* out of his head!

PREACHER WOMAN (*Weeping*)   It was necessary . . . to do that.

BECLCH (*Hooking her arm around the* PREACHER WOMAN's *neck in a choking hold*)   Call Uncle! Call Uncle! Oooo you antagonize me! You antagonize me!

NUALA (*Excited*)   Ooo a little bit of food came out of her mouth—ooo her face looks like a rubber bag!

BECLCH (*Choking the* PREACHER WOMAN)   Call Uncle! Call Uncle! A lot better a lot worse! A lot better a lot worse! Is this a lot better or a lot—worse?

> (BECLCH *flings the body from her. She gasps for breath, pauses and leaves.* YAGO, *who had been watching, goes to help* MANK *and* NUALA *drag the bodies out*)

SCENE 2

In the bar; BECLCH *and* JOSE *are sitting at a table. The* BARTENDER *and* CUSTOMER *are somewhere offstage.*

BECLCH (*Matter-of-factly*)   I eat my peck of dirt just like everybody else. (*Leans toward* JOSE, *admiringly*) Boy, do you have big forearms! (*Smiles and drinks*) Really first-rate forearms! (*Pause*) I hate fat hands!

JOSE (*Indignant*)   I don't have fat hands!

BECLCH (*Coyly*)   I know you don't. (Leans toward him) Boy, could you make *me* happy! (*Pause*) I want to touch your neck!

JOSE (*Smiling*)   Why?

BECLCH (*Strokes his neck*)   I love your neck! (*Very sexy*) I could kill for you—I could climb up a gumtree for you!

JOSE (*Boyishly*)   I really like you!

BECLCH (*Tenderly*)   I'm glad because I *really* like you, too . . . I'm a warm person and I think you are, too. I know you are! People like us have to be careful—all the evil in the world might get to us, give us the jitters— if we're not careful. (*Excited*) Let's be careful!

(*She kisses him*)

94

JOSE (*Pleased*)   Sure, Beclch.

BECLCH (*Girlish*)   Call me baby— Say, "Sure, baby."

JOSE (*Soft, sexy*)   Sure, baby.

BECLCH (*Exuberant*)   I'm so joyful with you, Jose! (*Pause*)
And I love your name!

JOSE (*Happy*)   I like your name—Beclch! Beclch! Beclch
—what's your last name?

BECLCH   I don't have one.

JOSE   Everybody's got a last name.

BECLCH (*Smiling*)   Not me. And you want to know something? I'm glad that I don't have one—a last name.

JOSE   Why?

BECLCH   Simpler to have one name—safer! Then we really
know who we are.

JOSE (*Warmly*)   I really like you, baby.

BECLCH (*Smiling*)   Because I'm eccentric?

JOSE   Yes—I like that!

BECLCH   Jose—how *I hope* your soul never becomes
splotched up!

JOSE   It won't.

BECLCH (*Tremulous*)   O it might!

JOSE (*Takes her hand*)   No, it won't. You're so gentle,
tender.

BECLCH   You are too, dear Jose. (*They gaze at each other;
pause*) We're both so full of love. (*Eagerly*) Let's always
be that way—so full of love! (*Seriously*) Let's never de-
grade anything—anyone—ourselves.

JOSE (*Quietly*) Never, baby, never. (*Pause*) I once did . . . something bad.

BECLCH What?

JOSE I shot a bird. (*Smiling a little*) But I wanted to . . . see if I could. And then I cried.

BECLCH (*Tenderly*) "I could not love thee, dear, so much, loved I not honor more." You're sensitive . . . sweet Jose, you're *so* sensitive.

JOSE Am I, baby?

BECLCH O yes! And you've got *so much* passion. (*Pause*) You've got such big hands.

(BECLCH *smiles and kisses his hand*)

JOSE (*Smiling, a little proud*) They say that's a sign of virility . . . big hands, big feet.

BECLCH (*Amused*) No, sweet Jose . . . that's a myth.

JOSE That's what they say.

BECLCH (*Holding his hand close to her mouth, softly*) It's a myth . . . just a myth. (*Pause. Moved by him, she speaks eagerly*) O Jose, promise me that you'll never gyp yourself!

JOSE Gyp myself! What?

BECLCH (*Very serious*) I mean—never cheat yourself of living—never become *stringy and mewing!*

JOSE (*Not understanding her, vaguely*) Stringy, mewing . . .

BECLCH Weak . . . I mean weak. (*Pause*) I don't want you to end up being stuffed in a barrel!

(*Moved,* BECLCH *catches her breath*)

JOSE (*Trying to calm her*) I'm not going to be stuffed in a barrel, baby.

BECLCH I want you to always be like a—bobolink!

JOSE (*Throaty*) Baby, I'm starting to erect.

BECLCH (*Quietly*) Good . . . that's nature. (*Smiling*) We must not alter nature. (*Becoming serious*) The fat cats do that all the time . . . alter . . . nature. They're so cunning!

JOSE (*Amused*) Who, baby?

BECLCH The fat cats—you know, most people! They're so hostile, hateful—but they won't give us any of their grim torments!

JOSE (*Amused*) I feel kind of tormented now. (*Hotly*) I want to make love to you.

BECLCH (*Matter-of-factly*) That makes perfect sense . . . love . . . love is good. (BECLCH *tenses and pauses; she calls to the* BARTENDER, *loudly*) When's the cock fight? What time?

JOSE (*Bursting with laughter*) Cock fight! Baby, are you kidding!

BECLCH No. (*Loudly to the* BARTENDER) When are the fighting cocks going to fight?

BARTENDER In a coupla minutes, miss.

BECLCH Good. (*To* JOSE, *quietly, intensely*) Jose, don't think I'm a savage . . . but I met you here . . . in this bar . . . because of a thing that they do here . . . that happens here. Cock fighting . . . it's marvelous . . . and terrible too . . . but things happen inside us . . . when we look . . . when we bear witness.

JOSE (*Aghast*)   Cock fighting is so cruel!

BECLCH (*Gently*)   My heart breaks when you call it cruel. No, sweet Jose . . . a cock fight is not cruel . . . for me . . . us to see . . . it's simply an evil reality . . . that's all . . .

JOSE   That's enough! I'm not—morbid!

BECLCH   You are . . . we all are.

JOSE (*Vehemently*)   That's *your* problem, Beclch!

(*The* FIGHTING COCKS *enter*)

BECLCH (*Excited*)   They're here, love. Hold my hands— keep my hands warm with your big hands! (*The* COCKS *fight each other with two-pronged long forks. They scream in high-pitched sounds.* BECLCH *is very excited;* JOSE *downs shots of whiskey.* BECLCH *shouts to the* COCKS) Nobody wears kid gloves here! (*To* JOSE) Who are you for? I'm for the one with the fish eyes!

JOSE   I'm getting out!

BECLCH   No! No! Don't! (*Angrily, in a low voice*) A woman is suspect if she's alone here!

JOSE (*Getting up, groggy*)   I'm going to throw up.

(*One of the* COCKS *falls against the table.* JOSE *starts to heave and vomits in a corner. The* BARTENDER *goes to* JOSE)

BARTENDER   You better go into the men's room—this has gotta be cleaned up.

BECLCH (*Angrily*)   No! The puke must stay! And he's all right now! (*To* JOSE, *controlled*) Sit down, Jose. Pull yourself together, baby.

JOSE (*Half sits, half lies*)   I'm . . . sick . . .

BECLCH (*Gently*)   You drink too much, darling . . . Darling, put your head between your knees, it'll bring the blood back to your brain.

JOSE   I'm . . . so . . . sick—I can't stand the stink . . .

BECLCH   (*Matter-of-factly*)   Just vomit and blood, baby.

JOSE   I can't . . . stand it . . .

CUSTOMER   (*Calling to the* BARTENDER)   Hey, Dan—clean up the mess!

BARTENDER   (*Approaching the table*)   I've gotta clean . . .

BECLCH   (*Angrily*)   Leave it alone! (JOSE *collapses*. BARTENDER *stoops down to help him up*) Leave him alone!

BARTENDER   Lady, this guy is sick!

BECLCH   (*Coldly*)   I said to leave him alone! I know what is right for him—and get the hell out of my way! I want to see the fight!

BARTENDER   Your boyfriend's lying in puke—and you wanna watch the fight!

(BECLCH *ignores the* BARTENDER, *who walks back to the counter; she goes to* JOSE)

BECLCH   (*Gently*)   Sweetheart, I'm going to help you, now. Listen to me—I'm helping you all the way.

(*She starts to push* JOSE *to the center, where the fight is going on*)

BARTENDER   Hey, lady—are you crazy?

CUSTOMER   What are you doing?

BECLCH   Everything's going to be all right!

BARTENDER   (*Cynically laughing*)   Boy, you sure love him.

BECLCH   (*Breathing heavily*)   I . . . do . . . (*The* COCKS *stomp and slash* JOSE. BECLCH *and the two men just watch, fascinated.* BECLCH *finally gets close enough to help* JOSE *push himself away. She grabs a fork from one of the* COCKS *and stabs him, screaming*) You're the one I was for—the one with the fish eyes! (*The* COCKS *back away, expressing their fury in their movements*) Get out, you cocks—you savages! (*Laughs wildly; the* COCKS *exit. She tenderly strokes* JOSE's *forehead, calmly*) If it wasn't for me, baby . . . you would've been stuffed in a barrel . . . everything's going to be all right . . . Jose, I'm not going to bandage . . . your cuts, yet . . . we have to talk . . . you're not *that* hurt, baby . . . we have to talk . . . about you . . . and what you are. (*Pause*) O, baby—I know you *feel* a lot . . . you feel so much . . .

JOSE (*Moaning*) I'm . . . sick . . .

BECLCH (*Tenderly urging*) Ramble, baby . . . just ramble . . . I'm listening . . .

JOSE (*His speech is long and drawn out*) For two years . . . I drank . . . my . . . way . . . from . . . army base to . . . army base . . .

BECLCH Ahh, yes . . .

JOSE . . . in and out . . . of whorehouses . . . all over . . .

BECLCH (*Low-voiced*) Perfect, perfect . . .

JOSE I was a folk . . . singer . . .

BECLCH When?

JOSE After I . . . got . . . out of . . . the . . . army . . .

BECLCH Perfect . . .

JOSE . . . I saw . . . my buddy's . . . legs . . . blown off . . .

BECLCH You were affected by that, baby . . . and I bet you went out and got drunk.

100

JOSE . . . yes . . .

(*There is a pause*)

BECLCH . . . I'll bandage you up, now . . . if you want, baby.

JOSE No . . . it's nothing . . . the cuts . . . don't matter . . .

BECLCH I knew you would say that . . . go ahead . . . talk. (*Pause, gently smiling*) O . . . but baby, how I love . . . O, never mind . . .

JOSE No, tell me . . . what you . . . want to say . . .

BECLCH (*Reflecting*) How I loved the way your curls . . . bounced . . . (*Smiling, sad*) when you said, "I saw my buddy's legs blown off" . . .

JOSE I saw it . . . Beclch . . . I saw . . .

BECLCH Yes . . . I know you did . . . you see all . . . the time . . . Go ahead, baby . . . tell me more . . .

JOSE I . . . knew at a very . . . tender . . . age . . . yes . . . so very . . . tender . . . what it was . . . that had been . . . done . . . to me . . . but I never actually . . . realized it . . . or had any idea . . . I just knew it . . . before I even . . . began to reason . . .

BECLCH (*Reflecting*) Before you had attained the age (*Smiles indulgently*) of reason . . . perfect . . . perfect . . .

JOSE I shattered . . . the . . . world.

BECLCH Yes . . . you shattered the world.

JOSE (*Innocently*) Beclch . . . I wonder what . . . it would be like . . . to be a squirrel . . .

BECLCH (*Kisses him*) Fun, baby, fun. I want to bandage you, baby . . . it's no good to wait too long . . .

JOSE . . . no . . . no . . . it doesn't . . .

BECLCH (*Taking gauze from her bag*) I want to bandage you, baby . . . everything will be all right . . . You know, I'm going to help you . . . I am helping you . . . to change.

   (*She bandages him*)

JOSE No . . . no! Don't try to stop . . . me . . . I know what I have to do . . .

BECLCH (*Gently*) Perfect, baby . . . that's what I wanted to hear.

JOSE Beclch . . . why did you want . . . me to see . . . a cock fight?

BECLCH (*Smiling, gentle*) O . . . I don't know . . . maybe I thought you'd like it . . .

JOSE I . . . think I did . . .

BECLCH Perfect, baby, perfect . . . I knew you would . . .

SCENE 3

BECLCH *and* YAGO *are in the field, she is eating a persimmon.*

BECLCH Yago, I'm going to *sanctify* Jose—if it's the last thing I do . . . I'm going to *sanctify* him. (*Pause. She rubs the fruit over her lips*) Mmmmm, a persimmon is like flesh—you can hear it scream when you bite it.

YAGO (*Facetious*) And that's what you like—a scream!

BECLCH Who doesn't? (*Bites into the fruit*) I'm going to knock him off his . . . golden rocking horse . . .

YAGO Who?

BECLCH Jose—you shit-face.

YAGO (*Bitterly*) You're a fascinating woman, Beclch— you'll knock him off his golden rocking horse.

BECLCH I'm going to pull off his wings . . . and sew them back on . . . lopsided!

(*She laughs*)

YAGO (*Coldly*) You're coarse, Beclch . . . you're coarse!

BECLCH (*Mimicking him*) You're coarse, Beclch, you're

coarse! (*She tears a bit of the fruit and throws it at him*)
That should *brighten up* your skin a bit.

YAGO (*Cynical*)   So full of real human kindness.

BECLCH   The *milk* of human kindness—prick!

YAGO   You're fair and virtuous—like a hatchet!

BECLCH (*Laughing*)   Like a hatchet—like a hatchet!

YAGO   And full of goodness like a blood pudding!

BECLCH (*Laughing*)   A blood pudding! (*Pause*) I'm going
to *stain you* one day—you grapefruit rind!

YAGO   Anti-Christ!

BECLCH   I'm full of impiety—and you need it to flourish!

　　(*She laughs*)

YAGO (*Looking at her, intensely*)   I need—something . . .

BECLCH   I'm a *suc-culent* fruit. (*Enunciates "succulent"*)
Come here. (*He goes close to her and she shoves the persimmon into his face*) I'm natural and you're unnatural!

YAGO (*Angrily*)   Why do—why! Why!

BECLCH   Why do you stay with me? Is that what you're trying to say? Is that what you're *clacking* out! (*Pause*)
Because you must.

YAGO (*Pathetic*)   Sometimes I feel like the air is knocked
out of my chest.

BECLCH (*Crudely*)   See a heart doctor! (*Pause*) Come on
now—stop pitying yourself. Do the fork business on my
back. It'll take your mind off your troubles.

　　(YAGO *gets a wooden Chinese back-scratcher. He is
　　in a mood of obedience now*)

YAGO (*In a childish tone*)   What's the utmost God can do?

BECLCH (*Draws out the words*) Rub—my—back!

YAGO God?

BECLCH (*In a soothing tone*) That's right. (*Pause; she squirms around*) Oooooo lower—a little lower, Ooooo—now my knees itch—give it to me. (*She pulls the back-scratcher from him and scratches her knees in circular motions*) I wonder if it—was—the fucking persimmon—that's giving me the itches.

YAGO (*Parent-like*) You might be allergic to something in Africa!

BECLCH I never was allergic to anything, anywhere! It's probably you—your scabby fingers!

YAGO My fingers aren't scabby! Maybe it was Jose!

BECLCH No—Jose is as clean as a newborn's bladder.

YAGO (*With sickly laughter*) Do you mean there is no urine in a newborn baby's bladder?

BECLCH No—no urine—no piss at all. (*She pronounces it "A Tall"*)

YAGO (*Laughing*) That's good . . .

BECLCH (*Hands him the back-scratcher*) Scratch me! And stop laughing!

YAGO (*Almost hysterical*) I can't help it—you say funny things!

BECLCH Scratch me! And stop your disgusting laughter!

YAGO Okay . . . (*Trying to stop laughing*) don't do any-thing—bad to me.

BECLCH (*Mimicking*) I won't do anything bad to you. (*Pause*) Ooooooo I wish I could get rid of the itching for just a minute—itching—itching!

YAGO (*Childish*)   There was a famous saint who had the itches—his name was Victor! Saint Victor!

BECLCH   You silly turd! Saint Vitus! Saint Vitus dance! Oooo —that's what I feel I have—in another minute—I'm going to w-r-i-t-h-e. (*Draws out "writhe"*) Yago! Scratch harder!

YAGO (*Afraid*)   I don't want to harm your skin!

BECLCH   Scratch—scratch! Oooooo it's getting worse! Scratch it, prick! Get down to my white bones!

YAGO (*Afraid to scratch harder*)   I'm afraid I'll hurt you!

(BECLCH *grabs the back-scratcher from him violently and starts to scratch at herself. She falls and squirms around*)

BECLCH (*Shouting*)   Somebody! Some reeking sonofabitch gave this to me! Oooooooooohhhhoooo Yago—douse me! Douse me! (*He dashes off, gets a bucket of water and throws it over her.* BECLCH *lies still, breathes heavily; she pauses, slowly sits up and moans*) Ooooo, better . . . that felt like a throwback to hell! All that itching felt like im- perfection . . . laying its eggs on me . . . (YAGO *leaves; she lies down again, rubbing her body soothingly; she takes deep breaths, sits up slowly, smooths her robe, smooths her hair, turns her head to look back at the hut. She starts to speak reflectively with philosophical tones.*) When money is down you've got to be careful of appearance . . . (*She picks up a clod of dirt, puts it on her leg, then brushes it off with a swoop*) . . . a drop of shit on the forelimb . . . can be destroyed . . . it is necessary, it is virtuous . . . bad days, fair, dark, hard, soft, hot, cold, earth, heaven, air, none. (*Pause*) Kaput! (*Two native men run by in back of her*) Boy, do I love the Negroes. They're proud, they're proud—(*Screaming*) proud proud! Proud like eagles! Masterful! (*Laughing*) I would fornicate with a bunch of 'em! (*Calling after them, though they're already gone*) Hey, men! am I a horse or a sow? (*Pause*) I want a boy . . . a small boy holding a white . . . oily . . . skull . . . he and me would sit together and we'd scoff at it—scoff at the skull! (*Pause, turning back*) Little boy, come out of a hut! (*Laughs*) Or a bush! (HERMES *appears holding a skull. He sits next to her; she smiles at him*) You and me are like babes, babes in a wood, playing, playing with nothing in the back of our heads . . . except lust and scoffing! (*She pulls him to her and kisses his head*) Hey, I feel like a beautiful virgin! (*Kisses him again*) With a scorched heart! (*Exuberantly*) Lie down, child—I want to digest you . . . (YAGO *enters and watches her. She sees him*) What are you doing here? Where'd you come from?

YAGO From across . . .

BECLCH From across where? The Nile—you (*She enunciates*) but-ter-fly!

YAGO Yes, the Nile. (*He has a pained look*) O, my fingers hurt—my fingers hurt—from scratching you . . .

BECLCH Why don't you bite them off! (HERMES *laughs and beats the skull like a drum*) Hey, that set him off—look at him slapping out rhythm! (*Chanting along with* HERMES' *skull-slapping*) Bite them *off* bite them *off* bite them *off* bite them *off!* (YAGO *is staring angrily*) Don't you stare at me that way—that antagonizes me! Go jump in the Nile! Self-righteous—self-righteous . . .

YAGO (*With despair*) The world's sitting on my back, Beclch.

BECLCH Well—knock it off! Be a prick—and knock it off!

YAGO (*Furious*) Don't insult me!

(*He slaps her face*)

BECLCH (*Facetious*) That's painful, painful. (*To* BOY) Hey, boy—bite his leg!

(HERMES *bites* YAGO; BECLCH *laughs*)

YAGO (*Kicking* HERMES *away*) Beclch, you're an animal!

BECLCH (*Sardonic*) Write a poem about it!

YAGO (*Screaming*) You're noxious!

BECLCH Noxious. Very funny word. (*Laughs*) Do a dance for us, Yago. You're *loosely* built, do a lively dance! Boy, bite him in the leg again—it'll *stimulate* him.

(HERMES *bites him*)

YAGO (*Moving away from* HERMES, *screaming to* BECLCH) Hateful—you're hateful—hateful hateful!

BECLCH (*After a long pause, quiet, intense*) I've just thought . . . of something extraordinary . . . for you, Yago. (*Pause*) How would you like to be the chief of these people? Yes . . . you'd like it . . . (*Smiles*) they'd grow your *yams* for you.

YAGO (*Bitter*) I can't understand your humor!

BECLCH Simple as apple pie. (*Pause*) Well, what do you say? Want to be a chieftain? Best thing for you as long as . . . you're here. Yago, being a chief will give you back your *spine*—you'll feel *proud!*

YAGO How . . . how?

BECLCH I'll fix itall—(*She pronounces it "iTall"*) first we must swell up a leg! (*Pause*) Your right one.

YAGO (*Aghast*) Make my right leg swell!

BECLCH (*Pause*) Elephantiasis, Yago—elephantiasis. Some of the natives here . . . have that disease. They call it the *divine affliction*. (*Pause*) You should have it too—that way they'll accept you as their king! (*Pause*) Their white king!

YAGO (*Shaking his head*) It's painful, painful.

BECLCH Yes, certainly . . . like a rabbit stuck in the jaws of a snake (*Pause*) Yago, you'd be the snake—not the rabbit! Think of it, you, the power!

YAGO (*Innocently*) Why do I want the power?

BECLCH (*Sardonic*) It'll prevent your nerves from jangling! It'll cure the sickness in your urethra! Power will be like a mother rocking you in her arms!

YAGO I want it, the power. I would not be malicious though . . . or make my subjects ashamed.

BECLCH Course not! You'd be *real white* with them— (*Laughs*) get it? *Real white* with them!

YAGO (*Reflecting*) I'd be fair to them . . . my subjects . . . I'd have scruples!

BECLCH Scruples, scruples! I like the sound of that word. Yes, you'd have *scruples*. But we've gotta swell up that leg of yours!

YAGO (*Afraid*) It'll be painful, painful . . .

BECLCII It's the only way your subjects will esteem you! (*Pause*) It won't hurt you any more than my itches hurt me!

YAGO I don't want it, pain!

BECLCH (*Screaming*) Then your inferiority will drag on— it's going to drag on and on and on and on!

YAGO I don't want it, inferiority . . .

BECLCH Course not . . . you have it in you not to want it . . . inferiority! (*Pause*) Yago, you would have . . .

broad-hipped women attending to your *needs* . . . as many as you *needed.*

YAGO Broad-hipped women . . . O, I'd be kind to them.

BECLCH Then let's get your leg swelled up!

YAGO (*Troubled*) My leg swelled . . . up . . . the only way . . .

BECLCH The only way, the *only* way. (*To* HERMES) Call the women, son.

(HERMES *leaves*)

YAGO (*Childish*) Will it hurt?

BECLCH Not any more than the itches. (*Pause, dramatic*) And pain is an *illusion*—it means you have no *faith* in God!

YAGO (*Reflectively*) . . . Christian Scientists say that.

BECLCH (*Patronizing*) That's right, Christian Scientists.

YAGO Beclch, will you esteem me when I become the King?

BECLCH Esteem you—I'll-kiss-your-ten-toes!

YAGO When?

BECLCH (*Facetious*) When what?

YAGO When will you kiss my ten toes?

BECLCH (*Mocking*) Whenever I . . . meet you.

YAGO Why?

BECLCH (*Laughs*) Why what?

YAGO (*Eagerly*) Why will you kiss my toes?

BECLCH (*Sardonic laughter*) Because of your kingship! (HERMES *and the* WORM WOMEN *enter.* BECLCH *speaks to*

YAGO) Fantastic bodies of these women. (*To the* WORM WOMEN) This is the one.

> (*She points to* YAGO. *The* WORM WOMEN *go to* YAGO *and squat before him. They apply vivid-colored "worms" to his leg.* YAGO *screams. The* WORM WOMEN *and* HERMES *have sympathetic expressions;* BECLCH's *expression is one of excitement.* HERMES' *feet slap out a rhythm while he pounds on the skull*)

YAGO (*Screaming*) King! King! I'm becoming the King!

> (*The lights go out completely;* YAGO's *screams increase*)

BECLCH (*Screams*) The worms are getting fatter! Fatter! (*The lights come up.* YAGO's *leg is huge and splotched with purple, red, etc.; he has fainted. The* WORM WOMEN *leave;* HERMES *is sitting near* YAGO; BECLCH *goes to* YAGO, *then speaks to herself*) . . . Josc, Josc, maybe *this* should happen to Jose . . . maybe this is the way for him to get (*She enunciates*) sanc-ti-fied. Maybe yes, maybe yes . . . (*She stares at the leg*) . . . I'll bet it feels hot to the touch . . . (*She touches the leg*) . . . Yes, hot and very tender . . . yes . . . (*Pause*) It needs something on it . . . to keep it . . . ant-i-septic, ant-i-septic. (*Pause*) . . . Spit or piss . . . spit or piss . . . what shall it be . . .

> (*The lights dim as she gestures to a* WORM WOMAN, *who ritualistically squats over* YAGO)

Blackout

ACT TWO

●

SCENE 1

Some months later; in the field. JOSE *is a little drunk.*

JOSE (*Dangling and toying with his belt*) My belt's too loose—it should have another notch! I'm gonna make another notch! Notch notch notch her in the eye—(*Raises the bottle and peers into it*) Hi ya, Beclch! Where are ya? . . . She's gone, Beclch's gone, gone gone gone! I'm baffled, baffled baffled baffled in Africa! Baffled in Africa! Hah! Where's King Fat Leg? Unbaffle me, King Fat Leg! I'll give you a kiss. (*Sadly*) Beclch's with the King, Beclch and King Fat Leg are man and wife—(*A* NATIVE WOMAN *enters*) Hello, lovely maiden! Do you want to play in the grass with me? We could suck the juice from the vines together—African vines. (*The* NATIVE WOMAN *sits down beside him; he looks at her. Pause*) What a beautiful neck —your head blooms out of it! (*Laughs*) Your blooming head blooms from your neck! That's *nature!* (*Sadly; pause*) Beclch loved Jose's neck . . .

NATIVE WOMAN (*Smiling*) Tat's natchoor!

JOSE You spoke to me! Tat's natchoor, tat's natchoor, tat's wonderful!

(*He laughs*)

NATIVE WOMAN I speak` . . .

JOSE (*Delighted*)   Say it again, that, I mean, tat's natchoor!

NATIVE WOMAN   Tat's natchoor!

JOSE   Again, tat's natchoor!

NATIVE WOMAN   Tat's natchoor!

JOSE   Again, tat's natchoor!

NATIVE WOMAN   Tat's natchoor!

> (YAGO *enters, wearing king's attire; the leg sticks out grotesquely*)

JOSE (*Points at him*)   Tat's natchoor!

> (*He claps his hands*)

NATIVE WOMAN   Tat's King Yago!

JOSE   King Fat Leg! King Fat Leg!

YAGO   Shut your mouth!

JOSE (*Feigningly, pleads*)   Give me a piece of bread, King Fat Leg! (*Runs to* YAGO, *gets on his knees*) I want to dip it into my vodka! (YAGO *kicks him with the good leg.* JOSE *falls face down and kisses* YAGO's *foot tenderly, then jumps up, rubbing his mouth*) I've got mud on my mouth! Ugh!

YAGO (*Bitter*)   I could have your throat cut!

JOSE   I didn't mean anything—bad. I'm innocent as a lily!

NATIVE WOMAN   He, lily!

JOSE (*Laughing*)   Me, lily! See, me lily!

NATIVE WOMAN   He, lily! Tat's natchoor!

JOSE   Tat's natchoor! I'm a lily!

YAGO   You're a swine—an *imperfect* swine!

JOSE   No! I'm a lily!

NATIVE WOMAN   He, lily! He, lily!

YAGO (*To* NATIVE WOMAN)   Get away from the swine!

(*She giggles and backs away on her haunches.* JOSE *falls in front of* YAGO)

JOSE   A question, King Fat Leg! I've got to ask you a question, King Fat Leg! Let me ask you a question! (*Pause*) Is salt *food* or is it used just to season food?

YAGO (*Baffled*)   What!

JOSE (*Loudly*)   Is salt food or is it used just to season food?

YAGO   What are you saying—fool!

JOSE   Is it food? *Salt!* Is it a certain kind of food?

YAGO (*Suspicious*)   Why do you want to know?

JOSE (*Intense*)   It's one of the questions—I want to know. I've got a lot of questions—(*He's brushing off* YAGO's *foot tenderly*) Is salt food or . . .

(YAGO *stomps on his hand and glares*)

YAGO   Food! Fool! It's a food!

JOSE (*Humbly*)   You know a lot, King Fat Leg—a lot. (*He sits down, rubs at his hand, and dangles his belt; he talks in a sing-song*) Carrots, eggs, rabbits, turnips, apples, intestine, nougat, flowers, oranges, olives, dates, salt!

YAGO (*Mutters*)   Crazy!

JOSE (*Sing-song*)   Carrots, eggs, rabbits, turnips, apples, intestine, nougat, flowers, oranges, olives, dates, *salt!* (*Exuberant*) I would give all those foods to Queen Beclch!

YAGO (*Laughs and kicks at him*)   Give all those foods to Queen Beclch, hah! Would you—and why? Why would you give all those foods to Queen Beclch?

JOSE (*Joyful*) Because I love Queen Beclch!

YAGO (*Facetious*) Love Queen Beclch, do you—and why?

JOSE (*Exuberant*) She's god-made! Beclch's god-made! (*Pause*) You're certain salt is food?

YAGO Certainly, swine! I'll prove it to you! Here, woman! (*The* NATIVE WOMAN *crawls to him*) Let me see your fingernails. (*He takes her hands and studies them*) Long, nice and long, almost as long as mine. (*Pause*) Scratch his hand, woman!

NATIVE WOMAN Scratch?

YAGO (*Nodding yes*) Scratch his hand! Let it bleed! (JOSE *is more surprised than hurt as the* NATIVE WOMAN *digs with a finger at his hand*) Taste it, woman—taste it! (*She licks* JOSE's *hand*) What does it taste of?

NATIVE WOMAN Salt!

YAGO (*Smugly*) That is correct! (*To* JOSE) See? Salt is a food! (*Studies* JOSE's *scratch; facetious*) Just a small nick —not deep at all—and it *doesn't* hurt you—and you learned something—didn't you! (*He pokes his finger into the cut*) I answered your question and she proved my answer! Now, don't you think I'm a wise King!

JOSE (*Angrily*) Like hooey you are!

YAGO What did you say?

JOSE (*Jumping up*) I said like hooey you are! King Fat Leg!

YAGO (*Angrily*) Brave—feeling bold!

JOSE (*Screaming*) You're a fat bladder leg!

(*The* NATIVE WOMAN *giggles*)

YAGO I could have you smeared—like dung—by these natives!

JOSE You're a bloated nightmare, Fat Leg!

NATIVE WOMAN (*Laughing*) Fat Leg, nightmare! Fat Leg, nightmare!

YAGO (*He strikes her*) *Do you want to be brained!*

NATIVE WOMAN (*Afraid*) No brain me!

JOSE (*Scornful*) You're a bully, Fat Leg! A bully! Watch out—you'll turn into a cooked gizzard one of these days! These people will melt the wax in your ears!

YAGO (*Frantic*) I'm the King! I'll have your tongue cut out! I'll have you smeared like dung!

JOSE Who will do it? Who?

YAGO (*Shouting*) My subjects! My subjects—swine!

JOSE Your subjects! Hah! Your subjects think you're a half-wit!

YAGO (*Frantic*) They respect me! They respect me!

JOSE Respect you—they are *mocking* you!

YAGO You envy me, you swine. You envy me because I rule with Queen Beclch!

JOSE (*Frustrated anger*) Queen Beclch really loves me!

YAGO Queen Beclch is *sickened* by you!

JOSE No, she loves me! Beclch loves me!

YAGO (*Haughtily*) She and I want to *destroy* you!

JOSE (*Bitter*) You do. But not Beclch! She loves me! Beclch loves Jose!

NATIVE WOMAN (*Angry*) Beclch loves Jose! Tat's natchoor!

JOSE (*Laughing*) Beclch loves Jose, tat's natchoor! (*Wildly*)
See—see! Tat's natchoor! Tat's natchoor! Beclch loves
Jose!

YAGO (*Shrieking*) You drunken fool! You dirty cockroach!

(*The* NATIVE WOMAN *is very nervous; she starts to
chew her hair, makes wild gestures with her hands
and feet, and arches her back*)

NATIVE WOMAN (*In low tones*) Mum mum mum mum mum
mum . . .

JOSE She's terrified—you've terrified her! She's in a fit!

(*The* NATIVE WOMAN *throws her arms around, moans
and stares in hate, makes sounds through her nose,
breathes heavily. Sounds of tinkly bells and hissing
are heard from offstage somewhere.* YAGO *and* JOSE
are amazed. The NATIVE WOMAN *rises and runs
around frantically in circles, collapses and lies very
rigid.* YAGO *goes to her*)

YAGO (*Looking into her face*) Ecstasy! Ecstasy on her face!
(*Pause, smiles*) She's full of passion for me! Puffed up
like a blowfish for me!

JOSE Fat Leg, you're whistling in the dark—that's hate in
her face, not ecstasy!

YAGO (*Ignoring* JOSE) She's got bird's legs, very thin, thin
legs, bony.

JOSE (*Quietly*) You're going to die, Fat Leg.

YAGO (*Pretending not to hear*) She's got strong jawbones.

JOSE When you're dying . . . I wonder if you'll pass
diarrhea.

YAGO Full, sweet lips. (*Pause; he becomes aware of the
sounds*) Those sounds bother me! I shall tell the people—
not to make those sounds!

JOSE (*Laughing wildly*) You'll tell the people not to make those sounds! You'll tell the people not to make those sounds!

YAGO (*Exasperated*) What is funny about that?

JOSE They won't do what you want, Fat Leg!

YAGO (*Angrily*) If they don't do what I want—then I'll tell Queen Beclch! They'll abide by her!

JOSE (*Laughing*) They'll abide by her! They'll abide by her! Fat Leg, you're dumb, dumb! *You're in a pickle!*

YAGO (*Ignores him and turns to the* NATIVE WOMAN, *who lies rigidly*) You are *splendid* in your way. Do you know that? You are *splendid!* Some others might say that you're just a skinny black—but King Yago thinks you're *splendid!*

JOSE But King Yago thinks you're splendid! Fat Leg, you're the bloody end!

SCENE 2

In the hut; BECLCH *is lying down and being rubbed with oil by a* NATIVE WOMAN. *A bird's nest is sitting on a window ledge.* BECLCH *is looking at the nest.*

BECLCH (*Reflecting*) A bird bringing a worm to the nest, to put in the mouths of the little birds . . . sensible, sensible mama bird . . . worm meat in the bodies of the little birds . . . worm meat passing down the little throats. (*Pause; to the* NATIVE WOMAN) Get me some mussels! (*The* NATIVE WOMAN *brings the mussels to* BECLCH. BECLCH *handles and eats them sensually, ritualistically. She rubs some into her hands, then sniffs her hands, laughing a little*) Fishy. Fishy, fishy in the brook, papa catch it on the hook, mama fry it in the pan, baby eat it like a man! (*Laughs. Pause*) I want some persimmon, good with fish . . . sweetness and salt. Gimme a persimmon! (*The* NATIVE WOMAN *brings her a persimmon.* BECLCH *eats the top and then peels the skin back carefully, looking at it*) Thank God for my sucking mouth! Fish, fruit, I've got it all—I'm a regular big-wig, here— nothing could be better. (*She chews up some persimmon, then spits into her hand, looks at it, and laughs*) Looks like yellow shit—*noxious,* that's the word for it, *noxious!* (*Pause*) I wonder if persimmons do give me the itches

119

. . . but I'm not itching now. Nope, this old-fashioned girl is not itching now—I'm sweating, sweating in this hot air. (*Pause; she looks at the* NATIVE WOMAN) You've got good loins. You've hit the jackpot with those loins—no need for you to be quick-witted—with loins like that. You can be as soft and placid as you want—those good loins. (BECLCH *yawns, stretches and starts to chant*) Humming humming big humming huge song kind song drumming chanting and rhythm on the . . . earth. (*Pause*) I feel relaxed now—you can bring the sick in. I'm ready to cure. (*Smiles; as the* NATIVE WOMAN *leaves,* BECLCH *puts on an elaborate robe. The* NATIVE WOMAN *comes back with the other* NATIVE WOMAN, *two* NATIVE MEN *and* HERMES. *She gestures to them and they stand in front of her; the* NATIVE WOMAN *hands her a pot of honey and a stick*) Shall a woman's parts be laden with honey? Yes! Shall a man's parts be laden with honey? Yes! and a man-child's, too! (*She dabs the stick with honey and smears it on their abdomens*) Shall you be undone? No! Shall you know old age and decay? No! Shall you be weak as a little child's body? No! Shall you die? No! Shall the worms eat you? No! Shall your children and grandchildren know lunacy? No! Shall all your tribe know a sound mind? Yes! (BECLCH *gets on her knees, goes to each of the natives and licks a bit of honey off their abdomens. She rises*) Now go! (*The natives fall on their knees and start to back out.* BECLCH *makes a lifting gesture*) Up! Up! You walk out! I am a woman! You must never be on your knees to a woman! (*They rise and exit.* BECLCH *watches them, rubbing her body; she pauses. She lies down, running her hands over her body. The* NATIVE WOMAN *is sitting in a corner.* BECLCH *is talking to herself*) What do I feel? What do I feel? (*She takes some deep breaths, exhaling loudly*) Water gurgling in my body. (*She belches*) Persimmons . . . (*She sniffs her hands*) . . . I love the way my hands smell . . . what do I feel? (*Pause*) Smelling . . . smelling . . . I feel like smelling. (*She rises and begins to turn around in circles; humming*) Around and around I go and where my nose goes nobody knows. (*She goes to a corner of the hut where a pile of sticks is laid, and carries them to the center where she arranges them in a circle. The* NATIVE WOMAN *watches and starts to rub her feet back and forth.* BECLCH *leaves and returns, carrying a small goat. She places the goat in the center of the circle of sticks, ties it up and gags it. She places its neck between two poles, and violently squeezes them together. The* NATIVE WOMAN *goes to help her, and breathing very hard, the two women squeeze the animal to death.* BECLCH *pierces the heart with a knife, cups her hands over the wound and licks the blood from her hands. The* NATIVE WOMAN *skins the goat and cuts off its head. She places the head in the window.* BECLCH *cuts a piece of meat from the carcass, goes to the head in the window and places the piece of meat in the mouth of the goat's head*) Feed upon yourself, get your strength up. (*She goes to the carcass and begins to eat; the* NATIVE WOMAN, *who is also eating, cries a little.* BECLCH *rubs her hands over the carcass and inhales from her palms*) What good smelling this is. (*She becomes aware of the* NATIVE WOMAN'*s soft crying*) Drink some water, you'll feel better. (*The* NATIVE WOMAN *goes to a water jug and drinks*) I need some water—(*Laughs*) the kid's kidneys are salty, so salty—my mouth is parched. (*The* NATIVE WOMAN *brings her the jug;* BECLCH *drinks*) Meat and water, meat and water . . . good stuff to be full of . . . makes me feel affectionate. (*Pause*) O there's so much distress in the world because there's not enough meat and water for all the world's people . . . so much hatred . . . so little love . . . because of the lack of meat and water. (*Thinks of what she just said*) O I like that! (*Louder and preachy*) O so much hatred . . . so little love . . . because of the lack of meat and water! And there is a variety of enough good things on this earth, too . . . so that there should be enough for all! So that there should be enough for all! So that there need not be any lack! So that there need not be any lack! O my dear starved ones! My heart bumps for you! My heart bumps for you—all you savages! My maternal feelings are outraged! My maternal feelings are outraged—because of all that you lack! I want all for you that makes for health and happiness—(YAGO *enters;* BECLCH *sees him*) I want all for you . . . that makes for health and happiness . . . (*A little ironic*) Hello, Fat Leg, what have you been doing—sowing dry rice fields?

YAGO   I don't know anything about sowing.

BECLCH   Easy—all you do is pour (*Laughs*) your seed into the ground.

YAGO (*Looking at the carcass*)   What if the ground's too murky?

BECLCH   The murkier the better!

YAGO   Beclch, would you ask her (*Indicates the* NATIVE WOMAN) to go?

BECLCH (*Facetious*)   Why—you want to kiss me? You want to show me a scab or sore, an *inflammation,* you've got hidden someplace?

YAGO (*Angry*)   No! Questions! I have questions!

BECLCH   O, questions—well, they're inflammations, too. A question—could be a sore spot! (*Laughs*) Get it! A sore spot!

(*She laughs again*)

YAGO   You're drunk.

(*He waves his arm at the* NATIVE WOMAN; *she leaves, grinning and nodding*)

122

BECLCH (*Exuberant*) Drunk on the blood of the lamb! Blood of the baby lamb! (*Pretending to be tipsy, she picks up a knife and pokes it into a bone from the carcass. She holds the knife out to* YAGO) Here, lick! Bone marrow's good for you—very healthy.

YAGO No, thank you.

BECLCH (*Licking the marrow off the knife*) No, thank you, says Fat Leg. (*Pause*) I'd give you the tongue of the lamb, but I ate it myself.

YAGO Goat!

BECLCH What?

YAGO (*Pointing to the carcass*) That was a goat!

BECLCH (*Pause*) Yes, goat. Well, I ate the *goat's* tongue. If you had come a bit sooner I would have split it down the middle and we'd have shared it, Fat Leg.

YAGO No, thank you.

BECLCH No, thank you, says Fat Leg. (*Pause; points to the carcass*) Regular basket case, isn't it? An hour ago it was at its nanny's tit, and now pathetic—just pathetic! (*She lifts a chunk of meat with the knife and eats*) Life's a jungle, Fat Leg. A jungle! (*Laughing*) We bungle in the jungle.

YAGO I, I want to ask you a question. (*Screaming*) I'm forced to ask you a question!

BECLCH Well—force it back because I haven't any answers! (*She chews some meat*) I'm using my tongue, lips and teeth, now . . . nose, too.

(*She chews loudly*)

YAGO (*Angrily*) You're a barbarian!

BECLCH (*Cynical*)   Do I repel you? Do you feel an aversion to me? (*She flings a chunk of meat at his face*) Here! Chomp on that—chump! Rat-a-tat your chompers on that —it'll cure your . . . aggressions.

YAGO (*Angrily*)   You're supposed to respect me! I'm the King!

BECLCH (*Feigning concern*)   You sound like you're at loose ends!

YAGO   I am at loose ends!

BECLCH   Well, then chomp on a piece of meat! (*Dips a piece of meat into a glass of wine*) It's seasoned in wine for you. (*Holds the piece of meat out to him*) Here, Fat Leg, suck, suck on this juicy winey meat.

YAGO (*He bangs his huge leg*)   No! No!

BECLCH (*Laughing*)   Careful of that leg—it's going to bust open! All the corruption inside will spill out.

(*She gives a disgusted look*)

YAGO (*Screaming*)   Beclch, I am at loose ends!

BECLCH (*Not listening to him*)   Green pus and purple gore massed inside his skin.

(*She moans in disgust*)

YAGO   As my Queen I must respect—(*Exasperated at his verbal mistake*) I mean as my Queen *you* must respect me!

BECLCH (*Ignoring him*)   Full of poison—a bag of pus!

YAGO   Answer my question!

BECLCH   (*Finally looking at him, quietly*)   What is your question?

YAGO (*Desperate*)   Where's my power!

BECLCH   What?

YAGO (*Frustrated*)   I am a king! But where's my power?
I am His Majesty! But where is my power?

BECLCH   You're not making any sense! Where is your
power . . .

>   (*She eats some meat*)

YAGO   I'm so full of misery!

BECLCH (*Disgusted*)   And pus.

YAGO (*Sadly*)   And pus, too.

BECLCH (*Matter-of-factly*)   Bear up, bear up—don't get
glum.

YAGO (*Sits down and holds his swollen leg*)   I'm suffering!

BECLCH (*With a tinge of piety, reflecting*)   Long-continued
suffering . . . as a martyr might bear . . .

YAGO   The people don't listen to me—they don't obey me.
They laugh at me.

BECLCH   Love them that persecute you.

YAGO   But a king shouldn't be persecuted.

BECLCH   Shouldn't he? (*Pause; importantly*)   It is a fact of
the condition of being a monarch! (*Her voice rises*)   Per-
secution is a fact of the condition of being a monarch!

YAGO (*Bitter*)   Once you said you'd kiss my toes, whenever
you saw me—you said you'd kiss my toes because of my
kingship!

BECLCH (*Not listening to him*)   Yet even have I persecuted
thee!

YAGO (*Childish*)   Jose persecutes me too!

BECLCH (*Pause; looking at him carefully*)   Jose persecutes you?

YAGO   Yes! (*Pause*) And he said that you love him.

BECLCH   Jose said that I love him. (*Pause*) What did you say to that?

YAGO (*Angrily*)   I said that you are *sickened* by him!

BECLCH (*Pause*)   My King, you are like an open book!

YAGO   You called me your King! (*With passion*) Kiss my toes!

BECLCH   Of course, Your Majesty, of course!

(*She kneels before him and kisses his feet*)

SCENE 3

In the bar; MANK *and* NUALA *are sitting at a table. The* BARTENDER *is there.*

MANK (*Drinks; pause*) It's going to get rapidly . . . hotter.

NUALA It is June.

MANK (*Poetic*) Dancing and music go on—and the fecundity of man and beast—under the hot rays of the sun!

NUALA (*Pause*) That's not the only thing that goes on . . . under the sun.

MANK (*Slyly*) What else goes on . . . under the sun?

NUALA We change into (*Laughs*) pigs and dogs!

(*She makes a pig sound, then barks*)

MANK I didn't know you could make animal sounds. (*Pause; he leans toward her and speaks in a lewd tone*) You know, your head jerks up and down when you . . . grunt and bark.

NUALA (*Gives him a long look*) Do I look like something more than human?

MANK (*Laughs*) . . . a pig.

127

NUALA   Okay . . . now jerk your head . . . up and down. (*He jerks his head*) You look like a dog!

MANK (*He looks at her, pauses and leans back*) Ahhh, folk customs, folk customs . . . what would we do without them?

NUALA   Sit, drink and just get hotter.

MANK (*Poetic*)   Under the sun in June, sit, drink and just get *hotter!*

(*They laugh*)

NUALA (*Quietly*)   Something's got to break or burst.

MANK   Things have already . . . quite a few times. You know, she's got something up her . . . *sleeve*, now!

NUALA (*Facetious*)   Who?

MANK   The wolf! Beware of the wolf!

(*He howls*)

NUALA (*Laughing*)   Tell me, Mank, tell me.

MANK   Catching the pig, killing the dog!

NUALA   Folk custom?

MANK   Folk custom.

(*He laughs*)

NUALA (*Pause*)   I'm flabbergasted, flabbergasted!

MANK (*Grinning*)   About . . . what?

NUALA   That we're here! In Africa! With all the—savages!

MANK (*Leans toward her and grins*)   We're fortune hunters, Nuala . . . adventurous fortune hunters!

NUALA   I don't want my *head* cut off.

MANK Everything is a chance! (*Grins*) . . . if you're a fortune hunter.

NUALA I still don't want my head cut off—because of a *folk custom!* A savage rite! (*Pause*) The wolf's taking too many chances!

MANK Beclch is very adventurous. (*Pause*) I enjoy the *fun* . . . she sets up.

NUALA *And she sets it up—all the fun!* And she's taking *too many* chances! Making that dumb fool Yago, King!

MANK Fun is fun.

NUALA (*Contemptuously*) And you thank God that you're *part* of Beclch's fun!

MANK (*Looks at her, then drinks*) Fun is fun.

NUALA (*Angrily*) What if she wants to kill us for fun!

MANK (*Matter-of-factly*) Everything is a chance. (*Pause*) But that won't happen to us, Nuala.

NUALA How do you know that it won't happen to us!

MANK (*Pause*) Because somehow we always manage to do exactly as *Queen* Beclch wants . . . we know our roles, Nuala, our roles . . . and she has *no desire* to kill us . . . only to manipulate. (*Pause*) Nuala, admit it, you *like it.*

NUALA (*Angrily*) Yes, I like it—because I'm here—in Africa! If I was somewhere else I wouldn't like to do these things! The weird things, phony *customs she invents.* No, I wouldn't do them somewhere else.

MANK (*Lifting his glass in a toast*) Bizarre longings! Nuala, let's drink to Beclch's bizarre longings!

NUALA (*Bitter*) I've got some bizarre longings of my own, Mank—to feel safe!

MANK (*Facetious*) Safe. (*Dramatic*) I say *nay* to it and I toast Beclch and her bizarre longings! (*Leans toward her and speaks in low tones*) A few nights ago . . . she killed baa-baa, a kid . . . and later that night . . . she found out something that stirred around the licking fires inside of her. (*Pause; facetious*) That she's in love! That she's *pining* for a tenderness!

NUALA Grotesque!

MANK (*Laughing in high tones*) Yes! Yes! Grotesque! Grotesque! The grizzly wolf is pining for a tenderness.

NUALA And who does she want to put her bite on?

MANK Who does she want to stuff into her jowls?

(*The* BARTENDER *looks at them*)

NUALA (*To the* BARTENDER) Damn your eyes! Stop your damn eavesdropping! (*To* MANK) Who does she want?

MANK A young man—(*Facetious*) a stripling youth—he's got *curly hair!* The better to clean her teeth with!

(*He laughs*)

NUALA When will it happen?

MANK (*Enjoying this; he pretends that he doesn't know what she means*) When will it happen? When will what happen?

NUALA (*Angrily*) The . . . folk custom . . . the sacred rite!

MANK Soon, Nuala . . . I feel it in my toes and fingers. Yes . . . soon!

NUALA (*Drinks*) It should be good, it should be very good, (*Laughs, realizing his game*) You old bag of hairy skin! We should drink to it, to a new *unblemished* God-King!

130

MANK (*Laughing*)   Yes, an unblemished God-King!

NUALA (*Arches her back sexily*)   Mmmmm, I feel awake, elated!

MANK (*Leans toward her to kiss her*)   I can tell you're elated . . . your nose gets a *ruddy* color!

Low drumbeats are heard. BECLCH *is sitting in the field. Next to her is a wooden bucket of fish; a knife lies near the bucket.*

BECLCH (*Reflecting*) Nature's order is a . . . dirty deal, (*Rubs her nose*) all that growth makes my nose twitch. (*Pause; she lies back, leaning on her arms*) . . . That I might see you . . . and delight in you . . . (*She lifts a fish out and puts it down in front of her*) so much do I love thee (*She carves the fish up*) . . . *I am smitten with love* . . . and being by nature neither good nor wise . . . I never keep my passion in check. (*She eats a piece of the fish and looks up to the sky*) The stars are fiery! Like an animal's eyes . . . a female animal . . . (*Pause; in a reverent tone*) the pure white flesh of him, Jose! The smallest hurts show up . . . on Jose . . . like red garnets on his skin. (*Pause; she breathes heavily and speaks in tense passionate tones*) I am all wriggling nerves . . . love congests inside me . . . I'm tormented by my *feelings* . . . there are rapid forces with teeth, *digging* inside me. (*Pause; she touches her lips*) My mouth doesn't even feel . . . human. (*She hears movement and sounds*) Who's there! *Animal or human!* Shaggy or smooth! Animal or human! (HERMES *appears.* BECLCH *laughs*) Well—you

132

can certainly brag—you're both animal and human! (*She hugs him to her*) Ahhh, little Hermes, I could eat you. (*Laughs; pause*) You shall bear a message from Queen Beclch to King Yago! King Fat Leg! Tell him to come here! Right now! (*He runs off. She watches him*) Beautiful little thighs of little Hermes. (*Pause; she lies down, speaks introspectively*) . . . The severe directness of dying . . . I've caused many deaths . . . but the words of women are soft . . . velvety . . . and pleasing . . . (*Pause*) . . . Some men are half eagle . . . (*In strong tones*) they are the ones to grasp this earth . . . and rule . . . (*Contemptuously*) Some men are just . . . rats! (HERMES *and* YAGO *enter.* BECLCH *sits up quickly*) Want something to eat?

(*She flings a chunk of fish at him. He looks puzzled*)

YAGO I . . . I've just eaten.

BECLCH (*Pause; smiles*) Well, just being hospitable. I thought you liked fish.

YAGO Yes . . . I like fish . . . but I'm full now.

BECLCH (*Glances at his swollen leg*) Yes, you are full. (*Pause; she looks at his face*) Yago, would you grasp the earth with your toes?

YAGO My toes?

BECLCH (*Matter-of-factly*) Yes, would you grasp the earth with your toes? (*He is confused, but tries to do what she asks*) You're not *grasping! Dig harder! Dig harder into the earth!*

YAGO (*Weakly*) My right leg . . . hurts.

BECLCH (*Matter-of-fact*) The fat leg?

YAGO (*Embarrassed*) Yes.

BECLCH (*Coldly*) Yes, what!

YAGO (*Timidly*)   The fat leg hurts.

BECLCH   Whose is it? Whose fat leg is it?

YAGO (*Humbly*)   It's mine.

BECLCH   Then say it! Say it! Say, *my fat leg hurts!*

YAGO (*Low tones*)   My fat leg hurts.

BECLCH (*Excited*)   I can't hear you.

YAGO (*A little louder*)   My fat leg hurts!

BECLCH (*Looking hard into his eyes*)   I still can't hear you!

YAGO (*Tormented*)   My fat leg hurts!

BECLCH (*Matter-of-fact*)   And that is why you cannot grasp the earth.

YAGO (*Naïve*)   That is why?

BECLCH   That is why you cannot grasp the earth.

YAGO (*Pause; he gets angry*)   Well, why should I? Apes do that—I'm not an ape! Why should I grasp the earth?

BECLCH   There is no question of why you should—you must!

YAGO   Why must I?

BECLCH (*Sarcastic*)   Because of your kingship! (*Pause*) And you just spoke of the ape! The ape is a king! And the ape grasps the earth with his toes! (*Sardonic*) A king must be able—able to grasp the earth with his toes! It is a symbolic action that *tells* whether he is fit to rule!

YAGO   Fit to rule?

BECLCH   Yes! Yes! You should know this! You—who always want me to kiss your ten toes!

   (*She picks up a piece of fish and eats*)

YAGO   But I never heard of the symbolic action of of . . .

BECLCH (*Loudly*) Grasping the earth! Well, now you have heard of it! And you can't do it! And a king must be able to! (*She jumps up, stands with her legs wide, and presses her feet hard*) I grasp the earth! I grasp the earth with my toes! (HERMES *imitates her*) Even the child can do it! Grasp the earth! But you, the King! Cannot! (*Pause*) I think that you are . . . a rat . . . not *fit* to be King!

YAGO (*Screaming*) But it was your fault! It is your fault. You made me get my leg swelled up! You made me!

BECLCH I made you?

YAGO You made me get the disease! Elephantiasis! You made me get my leg swelled up!

BECLCH (*Pause*) I am a woman . . . a woman! How could I make a *man,* a king, do something—that he doesn't want to do!

YAGO I didn't want to! I didn't want to get my leg swelled up!

BECLCH Why! Why!

YAGO Because of the pain! I feel pain!

BECLCH (*Pause*) A king must not have pain. Pain distracts. A king must not be distracted . . . from his obligations. (*Pause*) You are not *fit* . . . to be King . . . the burden is too great for you to bear. (*Pause*) It is best that you are relieved of the burden . . . it is best that you are relieved. I made a mistake, yes, it's true . . . I influenced you to . . . get your leg swelled up . . . it was the only way the natives would accept you . . . so many of the men get the disease that it has become an affliction of *honor!* (*Pause*) But most of them . . . are able to bear . . . the pain . . . those who cannot are just considered miserable creatures unable to *transcend* the pain of the *divine* affliction. What manner of king could they have?

One who feels pain all the time? No! No! They cannot
be ruled by a cripple! (*Pause*) You will be . . . relieved
of the burden of being King! (*Pause*) Yes, it is too much
for you . . . you cannot stand it . . . you cannot bear it,
the pain . . . it distracts you from the duties of being
. . . King. You *cannot stand* the pain!

YAGO   I can't stand the pain! I put my leg into cold water
—I have women massage it—massaging it makes it worse!
Do you know that? I have the women fan it! It doesn't
help! I cannot stand the pain! . . . I feel nothing but
pain, nothing but pain . . .

BECLCH (*Reflecting*)   Nothing . . . but pain.

YAGO (*Whimpers*)   It's always there—it's always there.

BECLCH (*Tense*)   I can't bear it . . . I can't bear the fact of
your suffering. (*Pause; she looks closely at the leg*) It
looks a little rotten.

YAGO (*Bitter*)   Looks a little rotten! It's so rotten it stinks!
All the blood in my leg has turned into a big stinking
lump!

BECLCH (*Reflecting*)   Your heart and spirit are . . . wincing because of the pain you suffer. Wincing! Ugh! The
excess of pain that you've had! Your suffering existence!

YAGO   That's *all* it is—a suffering existence!

BECLCH   Then you must die.

YAGO (*Pause, weakly*)   Die! Why should I die!

BECLCH   It's the only right way.

YAGO   Why? Why?

BECLCH (*Angrily*)   Stop clacking why! You get me mad
with your clacking! Listen—do you want a *tinge of nobility*? Because that is all you will get—*a tinge of nobility*

136

to your memory—if you have the guts to kill yourself!
You gutless freak! Snout face! A tinge of nobility to your
memory is better than nothing!

YAGO (*Frantic*) I don't understand what you mean by a
tinge of nobility to my memory!

BECLCH (*Contempt, anger*) You've played the King, Yago?
You've played the fool, Yago! You've played the fool!

YAGO I did not play the fool! I played a king!

BECLCH (*Cruelly mimicking*) I played a king! I played a
king! Shall I wildly applaud you! (*She claps her hands.
The* CUSTOMER, BARTENDER, *the two* NATIVE WOMEN, *the*
NATIVE MEN, THIN MAN, MANK, NUALA *and* JOSE *enter.
They stand near* HERMES; BECLCH *speaks to all of them*)
Applaud the King, everybody! Applaud your King! The
King is going to die! He's going to fulfill his noble destiny!
Applaud, everybody! Stomp your feet, everybody! Stomp
your feet and grasp the earth with your toes! O we all can
do it! Grasp the earth with our toes—but our King cannot!
(*They all do as* BECLCH *says, applauding, stomping and
pressing the ground*) What kind of a king is our King?
He cannot do the symbolic action of grasping the earth
with his toes! He cannot grasp the earth! He cannot rule
his people! O weak weak is our King! O let him have the
courage at least to die!

NUALA (*Shrieking*) My heart's desire was always to be an
obedient subject of an heroic king!

MANK An heroic king! Heroic in his heart!

BECLCH O Yago has heroism in his heart! He's going to die
by his own hands!

YAGO My own hands? How?

BECLCH Strangle yourself!

(*They all become excited.* JOSE *remains quiet. He hasn't done any applauding, etc. He stands apart from everyone and watches*)

YAGO   I can't kill myself!

BECLCH   Yes! Yes! Strangle yourself! Strangle yourself! Nobilize yourself! Our royal Father, give your Queen and your subjects—dignity!

MANK (*Chanting*)   We want dignity! We want dignity! We want dignity!

(*The others take up the chant, and* BECLCH *cheers them on.* YAGO *is tormented and keeps looking around at them*)

NUALA   Fat Leg! You're a sick chimpanzee!

(*The chanting stops*)

MANK   He wants to swing and eat stringbeans! He wants to hang a gold cord around celery leaves! He's a chimp-king!

(*They all chant "We want dignity! He's a chimp-king!" several times. Then they stop*)

NUALA   All the King wants to do is squirt spit from his teeth! He's a chimp-king! He's a chimp-king!

(*She picks up a long stick and pokes his leg.* YAGO *screams*)

BECLCH   Helloooo my King! Have you had enough of our urging? Well, show 'em! Show 'em you have a tinge of nobility in you! (*She falls to her knees grossly, in front of* YAGO) Strangle yourself! Strangle yourself! And be remembered a thousand years!

(*They all chant "Strangle yourself, strangle yourself!"*

BECLCH *alone chants "And be remembered a thousand years." The chants subside and stop*)

NUALA   King! Your balls and sockets are coming apart!

(*She laughs wildly and makes an obscene gesture*)

MANK   We're your good-hearted subjects! Your memory will last everlasting in us!

(*He giggles*)

BECLCH   Strangle yourself! Strangle yourself! Do the ancient rite! Do the rite that you must die!

MANK   We can't have a blemished king! A king filled with putrefaction! A king of putridity!

NUALA   You're a king of pus! King Fat Leg, you're rotting pus! King Fat Leg, you're rotting pus! Strangle yourself!

BECLCH   Do the one gesture of power that will give a tinge of nobility to your memory! You wanted *power*, Yago! Remember, power! This is your chance to have power! Strangle yourself!

(*He weakly puts his hands to his throat*)

YAGO   My hands aren't strong enough . . .

BECLCH   O yes they are, my King! Your hands are the strongest part of you! Use them! Use them! Grasp your neck and squeeze!

NUALA   King Yago, you couldn't grasp the earth with your toes! But you can grasp your neck with your hands!

BECLCH   Grasp and squeeze! Grasp and squeeze! Grasp and squeeze! (*They chant "Grasp and squeeze."* YAGO *moves blindly, exerting all his energy, his hands pressing his neck. Finally he falls, dying. They watch him quietly.*

BECLCH *goes to him; he gasps, then dies.* BECLCH *looks at his face*) He's had it! Look at the look on him—he looks like he was boiled! (*Pause; she stands up and faces everyone*) All this what has passed . . . is a religious ceremony . . . and has a quality of healing in it . . . a quality of healing. (*Pause*) It is done! (*Pause*) We can say, that though King Yago could not bear the burden of his pain of the divine affliction while he lived, he bore mightily his way to . . . death! What man died so nobly? What man died so nobly! King Yago! King Yago! (*Pause*) It is done! (*Pause*) One more thing—a tree rots! But a new tree comes! (*Pause; she smiles and waves her arm in* JOSE's *direction*) What more whole and lovely tree is there than your new King! King Jose!

(*They all look at* BECLCH, *then slowly turn their heads to* JOSE)

SCENE 5

Six months later. MANK, NUALA, *a* NATIVE WOMAN *and* HERMES *are burying the mutilated carcasses of animals; sacrifices of* BECLCH's *"ceremonies."*

NUALA They were healthy and vigorous yesterday, these creatures.

HERMES (*Sadly walks around, then sits down moaning*) Zus zus zus zus zus zus!

NUALA (*To* MANK) What's he saying?

MANK Woe me! Woe me! He's sad about the animals, sad about covering them up with dirt, he's thinking about when he fed them—now they're full of bite marks, rot and fungus. He remembers when they were all whole and skipping in the sun!

NUALA That's poetic! All whole and skipping in the sun!

MANK One little animal likes another little animal whole and skipping in the sun!

NUALA (*Pause*) Mank . . . what do you think . . . Beclch and the King do together?

MANK (*Lewdly*) You mean, Nuala, when they *come together* as man and wife?

141

NUALA   Yes.

MANK   They chew each other. Beclch is *always* salivating and always has a sharp-toothed idea in her head. They chew each other.

NUALA   Yes . . . she probably uses a hunting tool on him.

MANK   Have you ever seen Beclch trying to get rid of the meat stuck between her teeth? (*Pause*) She uses very strong thread . . . And you know, Nuala . . . the King looks miserable.

NUALA   She's *spitting* on him all the time.

MANK   She's done more than spit.

NUALA   (*Reflecting*) Beclch's always delving into what makes people tick . . . always penetrating into things.

MANK   She's an earthworm.

NUALA   An earthworm does *good* to the soil—what does *Beclch* do good to!

MANK   You're in a virtuous mood, sweet Nuala. (*Pause*) Beclch conjures up unfunny horrors! (*Poetic*) Some say it's a foul vice—I say it's good. (*Pause*) ". . . if you consider God the author of your race, but he that with foul vice doth his own birth deface."

NUALA   Why is it good? Why should anybody want to . . . *deface* their own birth?

MANK   For a whim, Nuala . . . just a whim.

NUALA   Beclch would say that!

MANK   It's a heavy burden to do what one must!

NUALA   (*Sarcastic*)   Do what one must! So what makes one do what they must!

MANK (*Pauses; smiles*) Blood . . . in some it acts like a geyser, they're *flooded* with blood.

NUALA (*Sarcastic*) A blood urge.

MANK You can call it that.

NUALA (*Sardonic*) Jose has Beclch fettered with his contempt!

MANK That's what makes the wolf's eyes bright!

NUALA Beast's eyes!

MANK (*Delight, relishing*) Her urge is like an infection on the end of her tongue; she's always got to dip it someplace or other, to cool and soothe it.

NATIVE WOMAN Queen Beclch is full up with fog and darkness!

MANK (*To* NUALA) She's right! Beclch is full up with fog and darkness! (*Pause; laughs*) She's got a big place to kick!

NUALA You'd never dare to kick her!

MANK I'm acting the ruling buck! (*Laughs*) And I'll bet the King acts the ruling buck with the wolf—I'll bet he kicks her in the dark—and makes her bawl! (*Pause*) That's why she lets him hang around.

NUALA (*Contemptuously*) His precious gift to her is his . . . cruelty . . . that's the tune she likes to hear played . . . the frigging tune of cruelty.

MANK (*Gives her a long look*) Aptly put, Nuala.

NUALA (*Hatefully*) She can't help her depravity! It makes her content . . . for a while. She's a glistening cold rock with a mouth! (*Pause*) Ever see her suck on a kidney, inhale the urine smell? I wonder what's in her mind.

MANK   The smell of piss, Nuala, dear.

NUALA   Beclch's ceremonies! Beclch's (*Ironic*) circumcision rites! (*Pause*) Remember how Beclch danced through the village . . . how she pounced on the little boys . . . (*Laughs*) how she told their parents that she was a magic bird! (*Pause*) And they held the boys' legs open . . . while she operated with nine steady cuts! (*Reflecting*) The onlookers smothered the boys' mouths with their hands . . . to stop the screaming!

MANK   (*Matter-of-fact*)   That was us, Nuala. We stopped the screaming—and the next day we fed them boiled bananas (*Laughs*) . . . the boys were lying face-down with their heads on pillows of leaves . . . the blood from the penis dripping into cups made of leaves. The little penises were like red flowers . . .

NUALA   I felt jumpy later . . . thinking about what had happened.

MANK   (*Matter-of-fact*)   You've been sensitized by the tortures you've seen—that's good! One should share the pain of the other who is getting his head bashed in—if you can't feel somebody's agony it's like sucking air through a straw . . . a feeling of defeat.

NUALA   Yes (*Pause*) . . . but there's too much excess . . . sometimes . . . in one life.

MANK   Nuala, you're spilling the beans about yourself.

(*He laughs*)

NUALA   How am I spilling the beans about myself?

MANK   I think you're *bored* with the scream of pain.

NUALA   No . . . it's not that.

(HERMES *is looking nervously out. He has seen* JOSE *leave* BECLCH's *hut. He goes to the* NATIVE WOMAN *and whispers to her*)

NATIVE WOMAN   King Jose go!

MANK   Yes, he goes out at night, he has the right.

(*He laughs*)

NATIVE WOMAN   He go forever!

NUALA   How would you know that?

NATIVE WOMAN   The child see him! The child see him with bags!

MANK (*Laughs*)   Yes, the child see him with bags.

(*He laughs*)

NATIVE WOMAN   It's true! The child tell the true!

MANK (*To* HERMES)   Did you see King Jose leave with bags? What kind of bags?

(*He laughs*)

HERMES   His things in bags! King Jose leave for good! King Jose leave Queen Beclch!

MANK   So the prime mammal is saving his skin from the wolf's jaws.

HERMES   Queen Beclch crying!

MANK   The time when good Queen Beclch would cry is when there would be no more meat to eat in this world.

HERMES   She love King Jose and he gone now!

NATIVE WOMAN   Very bad that King go! No good! People be angry! Queen Beclch cannot keep husband! People blame Queen and kill her!

MANK (*Laughs*) A rebellion against Beclch—a rebellion against the wolf! Because her husband left her!

(*He laughs*)

NUALA I told you Beclch takes too many chances!

MANK You worry too much, Nuala. (*Pause; to the* NATIVE WOMAN) And Beclch is God-made! She can't be killed!

NATIVE WOMAN She be killed! King Jose gone! She be killed!

HERMES (*Dancing*) Queen Beclch bleed from here! (*Points to his neck*) The neck! The neck! The neck! Queen be cut in the neck! We feed the head! We feed the head!

NUALA (*Frantic*) What does he mean by feed the head!

NATIVE WOMAN Queen's head cut off! Head sit on throne, bowl sit in front of the head. Queen's head eat from bowl.

NUALA (*To* MANK) Mank, it's coming—the hell is coming!

MANK (*To* NATIVE WOMAN) You are making Nuala uneasy, tell her that . . . no harm will come to us!

NATIVE WOMAN (*To* NUALA) You are gray spider! You are sacred!

(*She smiles*)

NUALA You mean . . . I won't be killed?

NATIVE WOMAN You are gray spider! You cannot die! You are sacred! Sacred!

(*She laughs*)

MANK . . . And me . . . nothing will happen to me.

HERMES (*Jumping up and down*) You are yellow spider! You are yellow spider! You live! You live!

MANK (*To* NUALA) We are objects of homage, Nuala. We are safe!

146

NUALA (*To* NATIVE WOMAN) You side with us! We are sacred! I gray spider! (*Points to* MANK, *who gives* NUALA *a disgusted look*) He yellow spider!

NATIVE WOMAN You are safe! You are safe!

HERMES (*Shrieking in delight*) You are safe! You are safe!

MANK (*To* NUALA) Beclch should be here.

NUALA (*In a low tone*) No!

MANK (*In a low tone*) She should be here and watched! You know she's tricky! She could make things very hot for us! The boy will get her. (*To* HERMES) Go—bring the Queen to us!

(HERMES *looks at the* NATIVE WOMAN. *She nods to him and he runs off.* MANK *and* NUALA *try to be casual. The low sounds of drums are heard*)

NUALA (*Stops pretending*) It's a lousy sickness! We're full of lousy sickness!

MANK (*Trying to keep his anger back*) This is no time for you to . . . suffer, Nuala.

NUALA (*Panicky*) We *are* in a mess!

MANK (*Ironical*) In another minute you're going to say that nobody was white with each other!

NUALA I can't fake it any more!

MANK (*He grabs her arm*) You better get control!

NUALA (*Frantic*) Mank, I was once ordinary!

MANK (*Low tones, deep anger*) Of course, you dirty bitch! You better get control—because . . .

(HERMES *and* BECLCH *enter. She looks very depressed. She sits cross-legged*)

147

BECLCH (*Pause*) I do need people, now.

MANK Yes . . . friends are a miracle for one who feels . . . low.

BECLCH I feel low . . . yes . . . I feel low. (*Pause*) You know he left me, the boy told me that you know he left me.

MANK Yes, it's terrible that he did that.

BECLCH (*Nods*) Terrible . . . How he swaggered out! I'll have that image in my mind forever . . . how he swaggered out!

MANK (*With a fleeting look to* NUALA) He's a young man . . . they . . . swagger.

NUALA (*Slightly shrill*) They have no heart, young men!

BECLCH (*Reflecting*) . . . His cruel . . . beautiful . . . body . . . High cheekbones . . . narrow eyes . . . so impudent-looking.

(*She shudders*)

NUALA It's true—they do look impudent at that age!

BECLCH (*Looking at* NUALA) At what age?

NUALA (*Nervous*) At, at King Jose's age!

BECLCH (*Reflecting*) Jose's age . . . twenty-one . . . young enough to be my own child.

NUALA You don't look old enough to be his mother! (MANK *glares at* NUALA) Your skin is so *fresh*-looking.

BECLCH (*Reflecting*) . . . Skin . . . Jose's skin . . . so beautiful . . . I'd leave red marks on his skin . . . after fighting with him . . . (*With wonder; reverent*) I was speechless, I was speechless when I looked at his skin, when I saw the red marks on his white skin.

MANK   He is very white . . . a little too fair for the climate
. . . here. It might have made him irritable.

BECLCH   Yes . . . he was so irritable. (*Pause*) I even think
I felt pain in my heart . . . when he was irritable. (*Introspective*) It *fascinated* me . . . the pain in my body
. . . that Jose caused . . . he almost coaxed pain to the
surface of my body . . . strange . . . not like my itches
at all . . . very different. (*Pause*) O, no, no—I'm exaggerating, I just *think* he caused me physical pain.

MANK   (*Carefully*)   I think it was a pain of the emotions.
You're a sensitive . . . woman.

NUALA   That might even be why you itch—you're so sensitive!

   (MANK *glares at her*)

BECLCH   Jose is sensitive . . . I am numb. I am a numb
beast! I want to cook flesh in fat and throw the gristle at
the fire—to hear the sputtering! (*She stares with wide
eyes*) I wish like hell (*Laughs*) it could yell! I wish like
hell it could yell! (*Exploding*) I'm a poet!

NUALA   (*Nervously*)   You are creative! Isn't she, Mank! You
have the makings of a great artist!

BECLCH   I've got the makings to tear—you stupid bitch!
Damn you, stop playing up to me! If I want a comment
of yours, I'll give you a sign!

   (*She makes a third-finger gesture*)

MANK   (*Wheedling*)   Thank you, Queen Beclch, for putting
Nuala . . . in her place . . . she can't help but annoy
. . . she's just a silly woman.

   (*He laughs*)

BECLCH   (*Angrily*)   You laugh too much! And nobody is just
silly!

MANK (*Nervous*) I was just using an expression.

BECLCH (*Introspective*) Jose and I . . . we were together six months . . . I wanted us to shine together . . . instead of being prey for each other . . . (*Pause*) No! I'm lying! I liked how it was . . . (*Laughs*)when he gave me ice . . . it was nice . . . he'd rub me with ice when I itched . . . it was nice. (*Pause*) . . . I tried to get him . . . to like liver . . . it's the best meat a young man . . . can eat . . . the best food for the blood. He wouldn't touch it! (*Pause*) He drinks so much . . . if he only loved the taste of liver, then even if he does drink a lot, the liver would have helped him to keep up his strength . . . that's reasonable thinking . . . but Jose is strong . . . he's very strong, now . . . he's only twenty-one. (*Laughs*) I wanted to fortify him on all sides! That's why I wanted him to eat liver . . .

MANK (*Carefully*) I love liver—but it must be just barely cooked!

BECLCH I'll eat liver cooked or raw—it doesn't matter to me—the texture of the meat is always different, if it's raw . . . it's one kind of texture . . . cooked, another kind . . . and the smell changes too. (*Pause*) Jose's flesh smelled so good to me . . . he smelled pure.

MANK (*Soothingly*) Like young green corn.

BECLCH (*Reflecting*) Like young green corn . . . that's what Jose smelled like. (*Pause*) I don't know what you've heard about us . . . Jose and I. I don't care what you heard! There was power between us like a link or an artery . . . it held us together . . . It was sweet and lovely like a blessing . . . sweet and lovely like a blessing.

MANK That's beautiful!

BECLCH What is beautiful?

MANK   What you just said, "Sweet and lovely like a blessing."

BECLCH (*Reflecting*) Yes, I counted Jose's eyelashes one
night . . . I have the number in my heart . . . and it's
my secret!

MANK   Queen Beclch, you are a poet!

BECLCH (*Pause; cynical*) . . . Because I've known love
. . . like mice and egg-laying things. (*Pause; laughs*)
What am I going to do now? (*Violent undercurrent*) I
am . . . cramped, digested, digested by my own lousy
lot . . . my course of life . . . I was up in the sky with
Jose! He was my own nervous system . . . you know, he
ripped me apart, he ripped me apart like the bit in a
horse's mouth! (*Laughs*) That's good—like a bit in a
horse's mouth—he ripped me apart!

HERMES (*Laughing*) King Jose rip you apart!

BECLCH (*To* HERMES, *gently*) Yes, Hermes . . . he did.
(*Looks at* HERMES, *puzzled*) Why did he go? (*Looks
away and reflects*) Why did he leave with his sweet
mouth? . . . He looked glad . . . sometimes when . . .
he was with me. (*Pause*) My head hurts . . . there's too
much heat . . . I feel like there's a knife under my
jaw . . .

HERMES (*Chants*) King come back in the morning he
scratch his hair back and kiss the Queen's head!

   (*He smiles*)

BECLCH (*Gently*) No . . . little Hermes . . . I know King
Jose won't be back (*Bitter*) . . . he's full of bad feeling
for me! (*Innocent*) Why is he full of bad feeling? Why is
he full of bad feeling? (*Pause; bitter*) I am not so thick-
skinned . . . that I shouldn't be able to know why . . .
(*In a low tone*) I am not a melon-headed female!

HERMES (*Chanting*) Queen Beclch's head sweet like coconut! (*Shrieks*) Head eat the meat! Head eat the meat!

BECLCH (*Looks at* HERMES, *then pauses*) Head eat the meat! What do you mean! Head eat the meat! (HERMES *makes a gesture of hacking a head off; he holds the imaginary head and sets it on the ground. She is bitter*) So I'll die and stink, finally! Very good! How? How will I die? It's not enough just to cut my head off! (*Pause; vaguely*) . . . But why will my head be cut off?

HERMES No more King for Queen!

BECLCH (*Pause*) Of course, little Hermes . . . no more King for the Queen! No more roses in the world . . . (*Laughing*) no more persimmons . . . no more love-sickened Beclch. (*Pause*) Ahh, once I watched turtles mating . . . (*Laugh*) they move slow . . . it relaxed me to watch the turtles moving . . . slow. (*Pause*) My lips will become black when I'm dead . . . like a dog's mouth.

MANK (*Cynical*) Like a wolf's mouth.

BECLCH Yes, like a wolf's mouth. (*Pause; seething*) It's not enough just to cut my head off! I've got spleen and an asshole and a fiery heart inside me! That has *got to feel beautifully, too!* (*Looks at all of them*) And who doesn't think so!

MANK And you've got brains, Beclch! You've got brains!

HERMES Queen Beclch's brains! Queen Beclch's brains!

(*He makes motions with his mouth as though he is eating*)

BECLCH So, you're going to eat my brains up, little Hermes.

HERMES Get fat on Beclch's brains! Get fat on Beclch's brains!

152

NATIVE WOMAN (*Grabs* HERMES *and slaps him*) You will never eat Beclch's brains!

BECLCH (*Violently*) Why? It's not the custom, or are my brains rancid?

MANK (*Laughs*) You're always humorous, Beclch!

BECLCH (*With tight control*) I am waiting for my agony, Mank. Think a little about that. (*Exploding*) And try to think about what I want done to this half-alive carcass of mine! What I want done before it stops feeling forever! I want to be punctured in every pore so that my blood rains from each and every pore—can anybody think of anything else for me?

MANK (*Carefully*) Flies might lay eggs in your wounds.

BECLCH Good, Mank. Flies will lay their eggs on my body like they do on rotten fruit—what else? What else?

MANK (*Lewdly*) While you are in your agony . . . things might be done to you . . . to make your body react erotically!

BECLCH (*Pause*) I'd like that, yes . . . a last voluptuous sensation of my gizzard! A *full-of-love* feeling . . .

MANK A hive of bees might be sewn inside of you!

BECLCH (*Laughing*) And they'll eat up all my *shiny* membranes!

NUALA That sounds pretty, Beclch. (*To* MANK) Mank, doesn't that sound pretty? The bees will eat up Beclch's *shiny* membranes!

HERMES (*Excited*) Membranes! Membranes! Shiny! Shiny!

BECLCH (*Pause*) I feel as humble and quiet, now (*Low laugh*) . . . as a sheep! The vipers are getting ready to rig everything up for me . . . my death. (*Introspective*)

. . . I hope I drool like an animal . . . I want to drool without making a sound.

MANK (*Pause; he leans toward her and speaks in a low voice*) If you make any sound, Beclch . . . it will be a horse laugh . . . loud enough to crack the dry earth.

Blackout

Istanboul

●

ISTANBOUL *was first presented on September 12, 1965, at the Judson Poets' Theater in New York City, with the following cast:*

(In order of appearance)

GODFRIGH   Michael Elias
BALDWIN   Henry Proach
ROBED MAN   George Economou
LEO   Jamil Zakkai
ZOE   Caroline Elias
MARY   Ann Linden
ALICE   Crystal Field
GERTRUDE   Joan Astley
ST. MARY OF EGYPT   Florence Tarlow

Directed by Lawrence Kornfeld
Assistant to the Director John Hendricks
Set by Malcolm Spooner
Lighting Technician Stephen Lamb
Technical Assistants Susan Blowers, Janice Saunders,
Simon Byun, Karl Herreshoff

SCENE 1

In a tavern in fifteenth-century Constantinople, two men from Normandy, GODFRIGH *and* BALDWIN, *watch* LEO, *a Byzantine dancer. A* ROBED MAN *watches; his face reflects the mood of the exotic music. Two Byzantine women,* MARY *and* ZOE, *watch also.*

GODFRIGH   He could ram my wife in the armpit!

BALDWIN   What?

GODFRIGH   He could ram Alice, my wife, in the armpit!

BALDWIN   What? What do you mean?

GODFRIGH   I mean if Alice was near him—look how he moves—some part of him would ram into her!

BALDWIN   Are you kidding?

GODFRIGH   Just let the schismatic try though—just let him try—I'll cut off his balls!

BALDWIN   O is that what rammed into her? He'd be a eunuch if you cut his balls off. It's no crime in Constantinople, the Patriarch's a eunuch.

GODFRIGH   He is? But that's not Christian! That's not human!

159

BALDWIN   A eunuch's just got scales where his cock should be.

GODFRIGH   He does? How do you know he has scales?

BALDWIN   Because I buggered one once.

(BALDWIN *and* GODFRIGH *laugh*)

GODFRIGH   I wonder if the Patriarch's been buggered, the Holy Father of the East.

BALDWIN   Probably—he's Greek!

GODFRIGH   (*Points to the* ROBED MAN) Always that same look, that same look of of . . .

BALDWIN   Superiority.

GODFRIGH   That's right! A look of superiority—like he could make gold out of piss!

(ZOE *and* MARY *give annoyed looks at* GODFRIGH *and* BALDWIN)

ZOE   Sirs, we are watching the young man dance!

MARY   Your voices are interfering with the music—it will disturb the dancer!

GODFRIGH   O we are very sorry, we are so very sorry. We are so new in fair Constantinople—we don't know just how to behave. (*Winks at* BALDWIN) But tell us, is it right for women, obviously high-born women like yourselves, to watch a man dance?

BALDWIN   The ladies back home, in our land, are kept in seclusion—very often with the belt and buckle on them.

ZOE   Belt and buckle?

MARY   Belt and buckle—a chastity belt?

GODFRIGH That's right—so we know that they might be faithful to us their Christian husbands!

ZOE But that is barbaric!

BALDWIN So is cutting off a man's balls!

MARY Ahhhh—but that is a different thing, hereditary titles are kept in families that way.

ZOE And did you know that some of our best military men are eunuchs? It's a myth that a eunuch has to get lethargic and fat! And they are very patriotic!

MARY Constantinople's eunuchs are indeed very patriotic! Indeed, the whole Empire's eunuchs!

BALDWIN Tell me, fair lady, are all the men in Constantinople eunuchs?

MARY O no, sir, not *all* the men—why just look at the dancer—he's as whole as any man might be!

ZOE He moves so charmingly—he makes me feel like I have drunk an elixir! O we must stop all this talk and watch the dancer!

MARY His beauty and vigor make me feel so happy!

GODFRIGH Mightn't I be able to make you feel happy? We could have some kebobs and hashish, then you could teach me how to dance, and then . . .

MARY Then what, sir?

GODFRIGH Then we could fuck.

MARY Fuck? What—what does that mean? I never heard the word fuck. I suppose it is a Latin word—it's certainly not Greek!

BALDWIN (*Laughing with* GODFRIGH) Let me teach you a song, ladies—a song from the West! (*He sings*)

I love coffee
I love tea
I love the java
and the java loves me
coffee and tea
the java and me
a fucka fucka fucka
fucka you!

(MARY *and* ZOE *try to sing;* BALDWIN *is enunciating the words seriously;* GODFRIGH *is laughing; the* ROBED MAN *has a cynical look on his face.* LEO *stops dancing and looks furiously at them*)

LEO (*Screaming*) You frustrated wild idiots! How dare you —how dare you teach that word to these innocent women!

BALDWIN (*Laughs*) Can't you take a good joke?

GODFRIGH By the Holy Father, the true representative of Christ—we were having a little fun—just a little fun!

LEO Is that what is called fun in the barbaric West? Teaching women lewd colloquial words—ignorant nuts! Boors!

GODFRIGH (*To* BALDWIN) Should I beat him? Should I teach this heretic-pig how to bow?

BALDWIN Christ's mother! Let's just take these two little ladies!

ZOE Take these two little ladies! O no you won't!

MARY You are boors! Leo is right! You are boors boors boors!

ZOE Rough and stupid—boors!

MARY And animalistic—boors!

LEO See—we know who you are! We Byzantines are sure of who and what you are! And we know who we are!

BALDWIN   We came here just to talk to some women and listen to some music—but you are making me itch now!

GODFRIGH   Let's teach the East, this imperial civilization— how to hail the Pope! But first I want to soften the bones of his face!

(GODFRIGH *strikes* LEO, *who deftly darts about blocking the blows;* MARY *and* ZOE *rush in front of* LEO)

MARY   (*Screaming*)   Don't you touch him! Leave him alone! Keep away from him!

ZOE   We'll climb in your hair if you hurt Leo!

(MARY *and* ZOE *embrace* LEO; ZOE *cries*)

LEO   (*To* GODFRIGH *and* BALDWIN)   Your kind likes to see women cry!

ZOE   Just me, Leo. I am the one who cries—Mary does not.

MARY   I do not cry because I am secure in your love, Leo.

(*She grabs him*)

ZOE   Do you not love me, Leo?

LEO   Mary and I are old friends, Zoe.

(GODFRIGH *and* BALDWIN *watch in surprise*)

ZOE   But I know—I want you to dance with me, though.

LEO   Mary and I are old friends. We want to talk.

(ZOE *clutches at* LEO. MARY *is clutching too.* LEO *has his arms around both, but he yields to* MARY *more;* ZOE *presses against him*)

ZOE   I think you must think I'm a . . .

LEO   Why do you do this?

ZOE   I think I'm going to cry again. Do you want me to cry?

LEO   No.

MARY   (*To* ZOE, *surprised at her emotion*)   You are romantic!

ZOE   I can't help it. I can't help the way I feel about Leo.

LEO   I know I'm sexy.

ZOE   O it's not just sex—a lot of men are sexy.

LEO   They are?

ZOE   But you have a sweetness . . .

MARY   (*Takes off her shoes*)   I want to dance, Leo. I want
you to teach me the new Syrian dance!

(LEO *and* MARY *start to dance*)

ZOE   (*Takes off her shoes*)   I have got my shoes off too, Leo.
I want to dance too!

MARY   Stop your ranting, Zoe! Leo and I are great together!
Just go away.

ZOE   You fat cat—I won't go away!

LEO   I don't like insults, Zoe—you've insulted Mary!

ZOE   I don't care—I don't care!

(*She screams and dives into* MARY. *The two fight.*
LEO *goes to separate them*)

LEO   You are acting like the Frankish women! Like cats in
heat! Stop fighting stop fighting stop fighting!

(LEO *cries; the women stop fighting and tenderly
look at him. They put their arms around him and
each other. The* ROBED MAN *watches them*)

164

SCENE 2

In the bedroom of GODFRIGH's *wife,* ALICE. *She is with her friend,* GERTRUDE.

ALICE Sometimes when Godfrigh was so lightheaded from the mead—he'd tell his filthy jokes—and then he'd begin to stare—at my armpits!

GERTRUDE Maybe he had a thing with armpits. Did he tell jokes about armpits?

ALICE Yes! All of them, evil jokes!

GERTRUDE Tell one!

ALICE You mean one of his armpit jokes?

GERTRUDE Yes!

ALICE O it's stupid! Well—but it's so stupid! I could never understand why it was so funny to him. One time there was a woman who was all lopsided. Her ears were set wrongly and her nose was where her mouth should be and vice-versa. So this woman went to bed with a man and when she undressed the man laughed and she got angry and she said if you don't stop your laughing I'll pee on you, whereupon she lifted up her arm and peed on him.

GERTRUDE   Bizarre!

ALICE   Yes, I think so too! You know, he never wanted me to shave my legs! I am not a hairy woman . . .

GERTRUDE   I am not either.

ALICE   But the little I do have, he said that I should keep —I didn't like that! I like my legs to be smooth!

GERTRUDE   Me too.

ALICE   He'd tell me about the Byzantine women and how hairy some of them were—and how it made him hot to think about them.

GERTRUDE   Ugh!

ALICE   (*Bitterly*)   He never appreciated my smoothness.

GERTRUDE   I hear some of these Eastern women rub chalk on their bellies to make them whiter!

ALICE   I am not at all surprised, they do and know a lot of ways to please a man—and then after forty years of fucking and sucking—they join a convent—become nuns!

GERTRUDE   They are a superstitious bunch.

ALICE   And their murky intrigues! Their rotten double-dealings. The Empress Irene putting out the eyes of her own son!

GERTRUDE   And they look down on us! We are called the barbarians!

ALICE   I hate the guts of Constantinople! I knew a Bulgar man once—and he said that Constantinople and the whole empire would be destroyed by God!

GERTRUDE   Like Sodom and Gomorrah!

ALICE   Now *some* of the Byzantine men are quite nice, though—they have a sweetness.

166

GERTRUDE   I guess there's always some good among the bad
—It's the women I hate!

ALICE   The men have a feeling for spirituality, I think. They
are different from our men of the West.

GERTRUDE   And they have such beautiful eyes and such
charming manners. And how they dance! And I've never
seen one drunk!

ALICE   Yes—the men are quite nice. One of them once said
to me, his name is Leo, "Alice, you chew food like a
woman, your jaw moves so beautifully as you chew."
We were having dinner of roasted lamb, when he said
that. "Alice, I am deathless when I am near you," he said.

GERTRUDE   Lovely, lovely—that's something Godfrigh would
never think of saying—that's poetry!

ALICE   His face is so beautiful, Leo's. Do you know he
modeled for one of the great Armenian artists? He was
Saint George with a golden halo around his head—his
sweetness.

GERTRUDE   I like a man to be sweet.

ALICE   Well, Leo is very sweet—he's ninety-nine and three
quarters percent why I am able to go on living in Constantinople. If it weren't for him I'd have made Godfrigh
send me home a long time ago. Do you know that when
I first met Leo—during one of our little talks—he looked
at me and said that he imagined my belly as being as
smooth as the statue of Aphrodite. Leo never said it, but
I think he doesn't like hairy women—the opposite of
Godfrigh, who thinks the hairier the better!

GERTRUDE   Perverted, perverted!

ALICE   One time Godfrigh made me wear a pair of little
Slavic fur pants!

GERTRUDE   To keep you warm?

ALICE   To get him hot!

GERTRUDE   Weird, weird!

ALICE   Hair, fur, fuzzy things, and he bragged about it—
he said a man should be unique!

GERTRUDE   A pair of little Slavic fur pants—and that made
him hot—when *you* wore it?

ALICE   O, yes.

GERTRUDE   No wonder he won't leave Byzantium—all these
hairy women around!

ALICE   That's right, plus the fact he thinks he might be able
to get rich here. Then he'll go to Jerusalem on a pilgrimage—and get his sins forgiven!

GERTRUDE   O no, not that again! I've heard that story a hundred times—they all say it, all the knights—that they'll
fight the Saracens for the sake of the Holy City—but they
never go!

ALICE   Why should they? Here is where the fun and riches
are! Hypocrites, what hypocrites! Jerusalem is always a
pretext for getting to Constantinople!

GERTRUDE   Nothing like a holy reason for a sinning need.
By the way, where is Godfrigh?

ALICE   O, he went with Baldwin and some Armenian to one
of the provinces—about buying some shrine. A shrine!
Can you imagine!

GERTRUDE   A shrine? You mean, a holy place?

ALICE   Exactly! One of the eastern provinces—I forget
which one—is having a commercial boom; thousands of
merchants from all over the world are pouring in. God-

frigh thinks buying a shrine and some land would be a way—a good way—to get rich—you know—selling relics!

GERTRUDE   Ohh—well these Easterners are very religious.

ALICE   Religious hah! Fanatical! And they *love* relics. Give them a cruddy toe, say it came from the corpse of Saint Christodulus or somebody, and they'll eat it up with devotion! Any dribbling beggar might be a saint—as long as he's filthy enough!

GERTRUDE   Disgusting!

ALICE   These schismatics are no better than Moslems or Jews! Gertrude, I really must attend to some business now . . .

GERTRUDE   Of course—I have visited much too long already. Adieu.

ALICE   Adieu. (GERTRUDE *exits.* ALICE *takes off her dress, puts on a filmy thing, and primps.* LEO *enters*) O my sweet prince of the East! I am so glad thou hast come to me!

LEO   I'm glad that you asked me, Alice.

(LEO *kisses her*)

ALICE   I love to feel your shoulders, your arms—and thou hast such beautiful eyes—as beautiful as a Turk's!

LEO   Humm, yes—it's the make-up. I haven't had a chance to take it off—just left the tavern a little while ago.

ALICE   How many women were following thee while thou were walking to me—three, four?

LEO   No women followed me, Alice.

ALICE   O, I've heard about thee—how thou hast all the women and the virgins burning for thee!

LEO   Rumors! Don't talk with thees and thous.

ALICE Why?

(*They kiss*)

LEO Because they sound silly.

ALICE Don't hurt my feelings, Leo. I want to use them—
it seems right with you. O, when I see you I cannot help
but know why women love you! I cannot help but want
to say the words from "The Song of Songs." (*She recites*)

"O to feel the kiss of thy lips
for thy love is better than wine!
Sweet to the smell are thine ointments;
thy name is as perfume poured forth;
No wonder the maidens adore thee!
O take me away! Let us hasten
that my King may bring me to his room.
There in gladness and joy of thee
we will extol thy love more than wine.
How right they are to adore thee!"

(*They kiss, and drink wine*)

LEO You know, Alice, sometimes women only want the
outside of a man—like his bone structure . . .

ALICE (*sexy*) . . . and his lips and his hips and his long
. . . eyelashes.

LEO I don't have a cloven hoof!

ALICE What do you mean?

LEO I am not just full of lust—and you do have a husband.

ALICE So?

LEO Thou shalt not covet another man's wife.

ALICE O sweetheart, I am coveting thee!

(*They kiss;* GERTRUDE's *voice is heard offstage*)

GERTRUDE'S VOICE Alice, it's Gertrude. I've forgotten my parasol!

ALICE (*Angry*) O—well—why did you forget it! O, never mind—come in! (GERTRUDE *enters, sees* LEO *and grins*) Leo, this is Gertrude.

LEO Hello, Gertrude.

GERTRUDE Hello, Leo—why you look like—why you look like Saint George!

  (ALICE *frowns*)

LEO I am not half as holy.

  (LEO *smiles*)

GERTRUDE I should hope not—and he was probably a eunuch.

  (*She winks*)

LEO And I am not.

GERTRUDE O I should hope not.

  (ALICE *gets the parasol and hands it to* GERTRUDE)

ALICE Well—here's your parasol, Gertrude—take it and leave!

GERTRUDE O I want to talk with you and Leo a little while —and I'm quite tired. I had to walk all the way home before I realized I was lacking something . . . my parasol.

  (GERTRUDE *gives* LEO *a sexy look*)

LEO You are not acting friendly, Alice. Gertrude should stay and rest a while. She looks so pale.

GERTRUDE I am so fair too. . . . O but I am faint too! (*She goes to the bed and lies down*) O Alice, I would love a little wine—this heat of Constantinople. Please, a little wine.

ALICE   No wine for Gertrude.

LEO   What? Of course wine for Gertrude!

(LEO *pours wine and hands it to* GERTRUDE)

GERTRUDE   Cranky, cranky Alice—poor Alice wears such tight girdles—they give her headaches.

ALICE   You didn't have to say that!

GERTRUDE   I wanted Leo to know the reason for your rudeness, Alice. When we know a reason for a thing—then we can understand it.

LEO   Is it the tight girdles that give you headaches, Alice?

ALICE   No! It's not the tight girdles! And goddamn it, I wear only one at a time! And now I'm not wearing any!

LEO   Alice—what has gotten into you!

GERTRUDE   Headaches, she gets headaches—they make her irrational!

ALICE   Irrational! You itching bitch! Get out of my bed!

(*She lunges at* GERTRUDE; *they fight on the bed and fall off fighting.* LEO *tries to stop them*)

LEO (*Shouting*) Stop it, mad women! Hashish-mad females! Crazy women! Stop it! Stop it!

ALICE (*Screaming*)   Get out, Gertrude! Get out! Get out! Get out!

GERTRUDE   Don't think I won't! You're sick!

(*She gets up, tidies herself and leaves*)

ALICE (*hysterical*)   Malicious obscene cat! Ohhhhhhhh!

LEO All right, pomegranate—I saw through her . . .

ALICE You did? Then why did you encourage her?

LEO O, I didn't realize . . .

ALICE Didn't realize? What?

LEO Well, women sometimes baffle me—I try to be helpful and then something always happens.

ALICE (*Crying*) O my nose—she hurt my nose!

LEO O poor little pomegranate . . .

ALICE My nose, my nose, it hurts!

LEO Yes, sweet one—your nose hurts—but it will feel better—Leo will kiss it.

ALICE O kiss my nose, Leo—make it better. (*He kisses her nose*) O I want some hashish, mmmmm, hashish.

LEO Leo will give his little pomegranate some hashish—in just a minute.

ALICE In just a minute! The blessed Virgin! My husband might be back in just a minute!

LEO He might? O the blessed Virgin!

(LEO *runs to the door*)

ALICE (*Laughing*) No, no Leo—I am pretending! It's exciting to me—to feel that at any minute—my husband might walk in! And find us fucking, or just about to!

LEO Pretending—you mean he won't be back any minute?

ALICE (*Laughing*) No, Leo, no— He's far away!

LEO Funny, so funny.

ALICE O I am not just laughing because of the funniness. I

am laughing because of the excitement! The excitement!
The excitement!

LEO (*Tired*) How many times are you going to repeat the
word excitement!

ALICE O, Leo, think of it! O I've thought of it so many times!
You and I in the act!—and then somebody walks in!

LEO First you talk about your husband walking in—and
now it's somebody walking in. Soon it'll be anybody walking in!

ALICE That's right, Leo! Anybody walking in while we were
in the act! Anybody would be very exciting—for me and
for you!

LEO Are you kidding? I'm not nuts! You know, I really
think you're nuts! I think Gertrude must have hurt your
brains and not just your nose!

ALICE (*Laughing*) Gertrude—now if she had come while
we were making love—then I wouldn't have gotten mad.
Anybody will do—anybody will give me this excitement,
as long as they have eyes to watch us!

LEO Watch us?

ALICE Watch us fucking! O don't be so innocent—people
liking to be watched is no *new* thing. The old Romans
watched each other like crazy!

LEO Alice, you are crazy! I don't understand—I really don't
understand you—and to be very truthful, I wish I were
in Egypt now—far away from you!

ALICE (*Grabs him*) O don't say that! Don't say that! Don't
ever say you want to be far away from me!

LEO The things you are saying—I feel as though ants are
crawling on me! People watching us while we're fucking,
Gertrude, somebody, anybody, old Romans . . .

ALICE   All right, Leo—forget it! Just some silly ideas—reading Ovid—he talks about things like that . . .

LEO   No he doesn't! Ovid never talks about being watched while love-making—and you know it! You just made that up!

ALICE   All right! I made it up!

LEO   Now why, Alice, why do you say things like that?

ALICE   Ooo I don't know. Darling, I'm tired. Don't be so critical—don't harp at me—just be sweet and hold me. (*Embraces him*) Leo, now sing to me—sing to me the newest chant from Syria. (*He sings*) Now let's make love —without being watched. (*They kiss*) Leo, have you ever seen Slavic fur pants?

SCENE 3

In a dismal ugly tavern. GODFRIGH *and* BALDWIN *are drinking wine; the* ROBED MAN *is there; soft music plays.*

BALDWIN If we don't get a disease by the time we leave Constantinople—I'll think it's a miracle!

GODFRIGH Why?

BALDWIN This place! This tavern is one of the filthiest in Constantinople! Why do we come here? Why are you always making me sit here with you!

GODFRIGH Don't put everything on me—you want to get riches too—you want to make an eventual pilgrimage to the Holy City too!

BALDWIN What has that to do with this disgusting place?

GODFRIGH I'll tell you—this place has a lot to do with what we want—namely riches!

BALDWIN O yes—and I'm Jesus son of Mary!

GODFRIGH Do you agree that the Armenians are the best businessmen?

BALDWIN Well, what does that have to . . .

GODFRIGH Just answer my question—are the Armenians good businessmen?

BALDWIN Yes, and so are the Greeks!

GODFRIGH Well, Beshar the Armenian—you met him the other day—said that if we really want to attract people to the shrine, we should have a real live saint!

BALDWIN A what?

GODFRIGH A living saint!

BALDWIN Yes—ahah! A saint!

GODFRIGH I am very serious. A saint to attract people to my shrine.

BALDWIN Our shrine! My money's in this venture too.

GODFRIGH That's better. Our shrine. The Easterners, as you are well aware of by now, are wild about holiness; they love convents, monasteries, nuns, priests, ascetics and saints!

BALDWIN Where are we going to find a saint?

GODFRIGH In this place—this filthy place. Her name is Saint Mary of Egypt—Beshar said she comes here sometimes, begging alms. We are waiting for her.

BALDWIN We are?

GODFRIGH Yes, but she must not know that we want to exploit her for commercial gain—otherwise she will never agree to come with us—she must not find out that she herself will be the draw of people's money—she must think that the shrine is her sanctuary and not a place of business—our business. We'll have lots of things lying around—bits of the true cross, pieces of cloth from the garments of Jesus and his apostles—umm, fingers, toes,

hunks of hair—Mary will go around touching all these
things—and people will buy anything that she happens to
touch! Think of all the relics we could sell—that Saint
Mary of Egypt has touched!

(ST. MARY OF EGYPT *enters, dressed in a hair shirt,
arms and legs hairy. She swings a bell*)

BALDWIN (*Whispers surprise*)   Holy Mother!

GODFRIGH   Son of Mary!

ST. MARY (*Chanting*)

Saracens never touched me—I hid
Saracens never touched me—I hid
Saracens never sucked at these teats
—I hid from them
Unbelievers never touched me
Unbelievers never touched me
Unbelievers never sucked at these
teats—I hid from them
Virgin I am—virtuous I am
Holy Holy I am, give money to Saint
Mary of Egypt the pure one
She who will get you in heaven
with a prayer! She who will ask
Christ Pantocrator to smile on you!
Christ Pantocrator who never smiles
will smile on you—because of Saint
Mary of Egypt!
Earthquakes swallowed up the Saracens
after they looked upon Mary's white
body—Saint Mary's still a virgin
so give her some money.

(*She goes to the table. The* ROBED MAN *gives her a
coin; she approaches* GODFRIGH *and* BALDWIN)

178

BALDWIN   Here, pure mother.

(BALDWIN *gives her a coin*)

GODFRIGH   Pray for us, mother. (*Gives her a coin*) Share some wine with us, little mother.

BALDWIN   Share our table with us—we who will go to the Holy City to fight the Saracen dogs!

ST. MARY   You will go to the blessed city and on the first day you will kill six hundred Saracens! On the second day, seven hundred Persians! On the third day, four hundred Turks! On the fourth day, three hundred monophysites! And on the fifth, sixth and seventh days you will kill all the Moslems and Jews!

(ST. MARY *gives long, gasping laughter*)

BALDWIN   Jerusalem for Christians!

GODFRIGH   Jerusalem for Christ's followers!

ST. MARY (*Breathes heavily*)   I'll sit down with you now,
eat some bread, drink some wine,
Christ's blood is wine, you know,
his fair flesh whiter than bread, you know,
his toe clutches the heart of the world,
the ends of his hair tickle the face of God,
wine, wine, the first drink I've had this
morning is this sip of wine,
bread, bread, the first bite I've had this
morning is this bread. (*Smiling, squinting*)
You are two men from the North, your eyes
are light like Christ's eyes are light.

BALDWIN   From Normandy, little mother.

GODFRIGH   We have come all the way from Normandy.

ST. MARY   With your wives? Have you brought your wives?

179

Constantinople's good for a wife, so many churches, good for a wife to be in the church, Constantinople's full of churches, wives should be in the churches.

GODFRIGH   Little mother, my wife is with me—and she is always in church!

ST. MARY   Is she an Eastern Christian?

GODFRIGH   No—for we are Western Christians, little mother. We heed the Pope.

ST. MARY   You're Christians all the same, West, East, Pope, no hope, who will judge the separation between East and West? Certainly God will, but we cannot with our human tongues say that we will judge whether the East is right or the West, I myself am a Greek though my grandfather was a Hittite, I follow the wisdom of the Greeks, I seek no sign like the Jews, ever since Christ saved me I wait to hear it from him, what the truth is, he tells me every night in my dreams, in my coffee cups, one time I turned my coffee cup over and I saw the image of God, he was in the form of a bear, but I knew it was God because there, in the middle of the bear's forehead, was the cross! A cross burning in the head of a bear!

GODFRIGH   A cross in the head of a bear!

ST. MARY   Yes, in the head of a bear, and I knew what it meant, a bear sways when he walks, his feet press hard the earth's floor, he is brown like the earth, he smells like the earth, and so I knew that the bear symbolized the world, and the cross symbolized God, and the world and God were one! And then when I understood in my heart all these things, a great wind came out from behind me, and I knew that a Saracen had put a devil in me, but after knowing what the cross burning in the head of a bear meant—I had been forgiven by God—and the devil went out of me in the form of wind!

GODFRIGH (*Screaming*) Saracens! We are impatient to get to Jerusalem! To rid the Holy City of the heathens!

BALDWIN How I must get to Jerusalem—to walk where the Son of God walked—to kill his killers!

ST. MARY His killers, the Jews, they had the chance to know him but they knew him not, they had the chance to kiss him but they kissed him not, but Judas kissed him with betrayal, kissed God's son with his evil lips, beware of red-haired men, they are the sons of Judas! I saw a red-haired Saracen on an Aegean island where I hid, I became very afraid because I knew he would try to kiss me if he found me, the kiss of betrayal! But he never found me! Nor did the other Saracens find me because I hid from them, Saracens never touched me, never touched Saint Mary of Egypt's sweet body.

GODFRIGH Little mother, you hid on an Aegean island, from the Saracens?

ST. MARY Pirates, Saracen pirates, but I escaped from them, God made one of the Aegean islands come up under me in the middle of the sea, there I was, the only one on the island, the Angel Gabriel brought me some rice and fish in a silver bowl, the rice lasted six years short of six months, the fish lasted seven years, God had provided for me until the Byzantines found me, naked I lived on the island, naked I was when they found me, covered with hair and dirt, my nails long as a dragon's, my teeth black like tar, but my breath was as sweet as a baby's!

GODFRIGH Did you say you were covered with hair?

ST. MARY Ahhh yes—this hair shirt that I wear was made from the hair of my own body.

GODFRIGH It is?

ST. MARY Ahhh yes—and you should have seen my legs . . .

GODFRIGH I should have?

ST. MARY They thought I was an animal so hairy was I—
I looked as though I was covered with black fur!

GODFRIGH Black fur! I would not have thought you were
an animal—I would have known you were a woman.

ST. MARY I did look like an animal, an animal with dark
hair, breasts, arms, legs, belly, covered with hair, dirty
hair!

GODFRIGH You never washed?

ST. MARY Never—it was my choice! Mortification for the
son of God! I never washed nor cut my hair, there were
sharp stones I could have cut my hair with, but I chose
not to for his sake! For the sake of the Son of God!

GODFRIGH (*Excited*) Do you know, Saint Mary—I love
hairy women!

BALDWIN (*Nervous*) O yes—hairy women are fine—but,
but Godfrigh, I think the little mother should know of the
holy place. The shrine!

GODFRIGH O, yes, the shrine. Because we love the Lord
and our Christian faith, the Lord has chosen us to do his
work, Saint Mary of Egypt. And so he has made a way for
us to serve him. He led us to sanctified ground where a
miracle happened in the tenth century. A cruel Turk, a
pagan, turned Christian, because of the love of a woman,
a Christian woman who became a saint so much like you,
pure mother. We have built a shrine on that holy ground.
But, alas, it needs the blessed feet of a child of Christ to
walk upon it, the holy ground. It needs the feet of Saint
Mary of Egypt! It needs the feet of St. Mary of Egypt
to press into its sacred earth!

ST. MARY The feet of me—ahh, yes—and I have got the

right feet (*Shows her feet*)—these feet. These feet fled from Saracens! I ran on them from unbelievers!

BALDWIN   Come with us to the shrine God has shown to us, for you! Make the holy ground it rests on holier!

GODFRIGH (*To* ST. MARY)   With your feet . . . (*Musing*) you have big legs . . .

ST. MARY   The biggest in the East! God gave me big legs so that I might flee from Saracens!

BALDWIN (*Nervous*)   Yes, the Saracens! But now Christians are asking you to go the way of the Lord . . .

ST. MARY   I always go the Lord's way!

BALDWIN   Yes—but to the shrine! The Lord has shown us the shrine—for you, pure mother!

ST. MARY   I like Constantinople—I won't leave—last night I had a dream—God came to me in the form of a giant oak tree and the leaves whispered (*Whispers*) Saint Mary of Egypt must never leave Constantinople, if Saint Mary goes from the city—the city will be destroyed by Saracens! I cannot go—I cannot leave Constantinople —I must stay to save the city! I have friends here, anyhow.

BALDWIN (*To* GODFRIGH)   Well?

GODFRIGH   What do we know of heavenly things? We are shown the Lord's way, and so is Saint Mary of Egypt. Who are we compared to Saint Mary! (*Softly*) Are they as big up as they are around the calf?

ST. MARY   What?

GODFRIGH   Your legs.

BALDWIN (*Angry*)   Son of his mother—Godfrigh!

183

GODFRICH Go away, Baldwin! I want to talk alone with Saint Mary.

BALDWIN (*Disgusted*) All right! But remember—my money! (BALDWIN *exits*)

GODFRICH Are they as big up as they are around the calf?

ST. MARY Bigger—much bigger—and salty!

GODFRICH Salty?

ST. MARY Salt is a purifier! I rub it into the hair.

GODFRICH Of your legs? You rub salt into the hair of your legs?

ST. MARY I said what I said! The situation is this—had the manna been salty, the Israelites would have died of thirst in the desert! But the Lord made the manna sweet—and so I commemorate the event by rubbing my body with salt—because my flesh is sweet—as is the flesh of all God's saints! His living saints!

GODFRICH I don't understand . . .

ST. MARY It is not for you to understand God's ways! Mysterious—his ways are mysterious!

GODFRICH You have salt all over you now? Rubbed into the hair?

ST. MARY Again I say to you, I said what I said!

GODFRICH Could I see it, sweet mother? (ST. MARY *extends her arm;* GODFRICH *looks, rubs his finger on it and tastes. Helplessly*) Salty . . . Could I touch your big legs?

ST. MARY Saracens never touched me—I hid, Saracens never . . .

GODFRIGH   But I'm a Christian! I'm a Christian! A Christian!

(GODFRIGH *falls groveling before her; his hands go up
her dress. The lights go out, except for a soft purple
light on the face of the* ROBED MAN; *his expression is
very cynical. Music plays loud and there is the smell
of incense*)

SCENE 4

The tavern in the first scene. MARY *and* ZOE *are drinking wine. The* ROBED MAN *is there.*

MARY   I loved Thessaly. Leo loved Thessaly—we fished naked on the hot days, after the fishing we would swim— what fun! O, he loved me, but that was a long time ago. I must be realistic!

ZOE   Do you think that Leo still loves you?

MARY   Of course! I know Leo—do you know he used to cry whenever I left him?

ZOE   Left him?

MARY   O, well—other fish, you know. Other fish—and I swam with them. Leo's only a tavern dancer, and I want more than just a tavern dancer. I must be realistic!

ZOE   Yes—you said that.

MARY   Leo is a child!

ZOE   O, but he's so beautiful!

MARY   Mmmmmm yes—he loves my body—he always went crazy over my ass, my breasts . . .

ZOE   Agh! You are vile!

MARY   O, go away! What are you here for? I'm the one who's going to be with Leo!

ZOE   I can sit here too! This tavern is for everyone!

MARY   Anyone—even for bitches like you!

ZOE   You're the bitch, Mary!

MARY   O, shut up!

>   (MARY *changes her seat*)

ZOE   (*Calling to her*)   You must have looked like a fat cow —Hah, swimming naked!

MARY   If you don't shut up, I'm going to tear . . .

>   (LEO *enters*)

LEO   Tear what—what are you going to tear, Mary?

MARY   O, it's Zoe. She's always trying to hurt my feelings! Leo, tell her to go away from us!

LEO   Mary, I just work here—I can't tell Zoe to go, just as I can't tell you to go . . .

ZOE   (*To* MARY)   Ahah!

MARY   (*Gets up*)   Well—all right! Good-bye!

>   (*As she is almost out the door,* GODFRIGH *rushes in and pushes her back in. He is drunk*)

GODFRIGH   I've got a hairy woman! Yaow! I've found one— come here, hairy woman!

MARY   (*Laughing*)   O sir, you are gay! O, I remember you —where is your friend? (GODFRIGH *grabs her*) O sir, you *are* gay!

GODFRIGH   Gay, gay—I'm going to kiss you!

(GODFRIGH *kisses* MARY)

LEO Let go of the woman, Frank!

GODFRIGH Aaaaaaaaaaaahh I remember you—you're the woman protector—a hairy-woman protector! (*He hugs* MARY) Hairy woman, kiss me back!

MARY (*She kisses* GODFRIGH) With all my heart!

LEO Do you want to be manhandled, Mary? By that?

MARY (*Does a bump and grind into* GODFRIGH) What's wrong with that?

GODFRIGH Hairy woman, you make me happy!

LEO (*Runs to* MARY, *pushes her away from* GODFRIGH) You fat whore!

GODFRIGH (*Blubbers*) Take a hairy woman away from me! Will you! Ask her—the hairy woman wants to be with me!

MARY (*Crying*) O Leo, keep him away from me!

GODFRIGH O hairy woman, don't deny me! Don't deny me!

MARY O Leo, keep him away!

LEO (*Shielding* MARY) This woman does not want you, Frank!

GODFRIGH Come here! Come here! Come here, hairy woman!

(ST. MARY OF EGYPT *enters*)

ST. MARY I am here, I am here, I was always here.
I was in the beginning and I am in the end.
I am alpha and omega!

GODFRIGH (*Runs to* ST. MARY) Two hairy women—but one loves me—one loves me!

188

ST. MARY   Saint Mary loves the Christians, Saint Mary hates the heathens, Saint Mary of Egypt knows a Christian from a heathen.

GODFRIGH   I'm a Christian, hairy woman!

ST. MARY   (*Breathes heavily*)   You're a Christian, son of Christ, Christ's son, fair-fleshed son of Christ!

(*She sits down at the table*)

MARY   (*To* ZOE)   Want to be friends?

ZOE   (*Smiling*)   We are always friends. Come here and sit with me—and watch!

MARY   (*She moves to* ZOE's *table*)   I love to watch!

(*She laughs*)

ST. MARY   Pleasure, pleasure, pleasure from Christian men, one from the East (*Points to* LEO) and one from the West! (*Points to* GODFRIGH) Man from the East, man from the West!

(ST. MARY *laughs*)

GODFRIGH   And you want a man from the West!

ST. MARY   I want what I want—Christ's manhood! Confess it! One of you has it! Which one is it, man from the East or man from the West!

LEO   (*Gently*)   Saint Mary has smoked too much hashish today.

ST. MARY   Saint Mary of Egypt has smoked and the smoke has gone into her, like the spirit of Christ! The smoke in me is the spirit of Christ! Who will deny that?

GODFRIGH   I don't deny that—Christ was in you!

(*He laughs*)

ST. MARY Saint Mary had Christ in her to the farthest end of the world!

GODFRIGH (*Laughing hard*) You're beautiful, Mary!

ST. MARY Saint Mary is beautiful, only the blind say naught, those with eyes see Saint Mary of Egypt's beauty, those blessed with eyes can see the work of the Lord! I am the Lord's work!

GODFRIGH Tell the man from the East what a good fellow am I!

ST. MARY (*To* LEO) Good—goodness sometimes comes from the far-off lands, the Lord is fair that way, he lets the goodness come over each part of the earth, spreading, spreading over, touching each of the Lord's creatures. The Lord's fair—he puts goodness into a man be he from the East or the West!

GODFRIGH (*Laughing*) And man puts goodness into a woman! I've put my goodness into Saint Mary!

LEO You have put your hands on this woman! You have corrupted one of God's saints!

GODFRIGH My name is Godfrigh! Put the last half of my name where the first is and the first where the last is! I frig God!

    (GODFRIGH *laughs wildly*)

LEO You have debased our women—and now you have dared to debase the saints of our religion!

GODFRIGH I've had only one—one hairy woman! Saint Mary of Egypt! The others don't like me—thank God for Saint Mary of Egypt, who loves me!

ST. MARY Thank God for Saint Mary of Egypt—she who

190

fled from the fierce Saracens—she who saved her purity from the rottenness of Saracens!

LEO (*Screaming*) But you let this Frankish swine spew on you! When the Pope's men spew on our saints—they are spewing on Christ! Saint Mary, he said it! He said he frigs God! Why have you let him defile you?

ST. MARY Against me—my name—there is no defilement! They rent Christ's robes—they swabbed Christ's lips with vinegar—yet there was no defilement! Like Christ I am! Against me there is no defilement!

LEO (*Screaming*) But you chose this stinking dog!

ST. MARY I choose what I choose. It is no business of yours —would you say to Christ—Christ, do not choose Saint Peter!

LEO But you are not Christ!

ST. MARY I should curse you for that! (*Everybody cringes, except* GODFRIGH) I should give you the eye! (*Sticks out her fingers in gesture of a curse*) I should make your testicles wither away! But I won't—dost thee desire me too?

  (*She squints and smiles cunningly*)

LEO (*Falls in front of her*) I desire thee to love me like a child—and pray for me—O Saint Mary of Egypt—Pray for me—forgive me! Do not curse me! Forgive me!

ST. MARY (*Smiling*) Ask the man from the West to forgive you. If he forgives you, Saint Mary forgives you—if he forgives you—I will bless thee!

LEO (*Crying*) Curse me then.

ST. MARY Thou art jealous of the man from the West! Jealous of Saint Mary of Egypt! Jealous because of love! Then vie for me, vie for me, fight for me—fight like Christians for the holy vessel! I am the vessel!

GODFRICH I don't want to fight. I'm tired.

(*He lies down*)

LEO (*Hands* ST. MARY *nargilah*) Hashish, Saint Mary of Egypt, smoke. I will dance. Mary and Zoe, let's dance for Saint Mary.

(*They dance*)

ST. MARY Hashish is good—I can dance better than those two—this hashish is good—I can dance better. (*She gets up and goes between the dancers, pipe in her mouth*) See what a woman Saint Mary of Egypt is! She can bless and she can dance! Hashish is good—my lips on my pipe, my limbs moving, my hair shirt itching me, it gives me pleasure . . . Constantinople gives me pleasure. The three of you, watch! Watch Saint Mary of Egypt dance! (*They stop dancing and watch her*) Again I say Constantinople gives me pleasure! I protect her always! That's a good thing—I save Constantinople from Saracens! Saracens! Lechery! Lecherous Saracens! Ahhhhhhh the visions! The sunshine on the dome of Saint Sophia! It sharpens the image of what I see—of what I see on the dome of blessed Saint Sophia—I see black lips—terrible black lips on the dome—it means—the black lips mean the Saracens! Ahhhhhh Saracens defiling Saint Sophia! Saracens stealing beautiful icons, holy relics! Ahhhhh I feel the stare of God on me now! Christ Pantocrator looking down on St. Mary of Egypt! Christ Pantocrator wants Saint Mary of Egypt to save Constantinople from the Saracens! Ahhhhh I feel the pain. (*She falls*) The pain of Christ's sores—Saracens are stuffing wool into Christ's sores—the wool reeks with piss! They are tearing Christ's body up with their teeth! Ahhhhh Saint Mary of Egypt

192

must stop them—must stop them from biting Christ. Constantinople must be saved! (MARY, ZOE *and* LEO *look confused, anxious. They leave. The* ROBED MAN *looks at* ST. MARY *and leaves; she lies still for a while*) I smell them, I smell the Saracens, sons-of-bitches, blood-suckers—they have sucked Christ's blood up—his blood turns black in their mouths. (*She sits up, sees* GODFRIGH) Here is one! Here is a Saracen! (*She circles him*) Pretending to be asleep—like Egypt pretends that God never cursed her! I'm not unseeing! Saint Mary of Egypt sees! Horrible Saracen! You will not ruin Constantinople! I'll squeeze gall and bile out of you! Squeeze you like the neck of a goose! Ahhhhh Saint Mary of Egypt's face burns! Is the sun shining on it? (*Her teeth chatter*) My teeth are clacking! The Saracen is doing it! He is making me burn! Lord, how do I—how do I kill Barabas? Ahhhhh my legs burn! My legs burn! Leg—It is a sign—I must cut off the Saracen's leg—evil—the leg is evil—if I cut off his—mine will be cool! (*Music plays loud and the lights dim.* ST. MARY *crouches over* GODFRIGH *with a knife and swipes at him. He screams*) I am cool!

SCENE 5

ALICE *and* LEO *are in bed, in an embrace.*

ALICE   Now say it slowly, s-l-o-w-l-y.

LEO   Godfrigh is dead.

ALICE   I'm embarrassed.

LEO   Embarrassed?

ALICE   Well . . . Godfrigh is dead . . . killed by an ugly woman. It's embarrassing . . . because I'm beautiful.

(*She stretches out her leg and looks at it; she gives a donkey-laugh*)

LEO   The woman is a saint—and don't laugh like that.

ALICE   A woman killed my husband—and I laugh that way because I'm nervous! I loved Godfrigh.

LEO   He didn't know how to love you . . .

ALICE   O stop it—you don't know anything about it! I don't want to talk about it—him—like this—but I must. Turn over and look the other way. Don't look at me!

LEO   Turn over—don't look at you—what . . .

194

ALICE   Please—my husband is dead! Do what I ask of you.
I want to feel you near me—but I want to talk—O I'm
asking you to move over—and look the other way!

LEO (*Tired*)   Yes—I understand you.

(*He turns away*)

ALICE   He liked this woman . . . the saint . . . to him she
was more perfect than me . . . I am conceited . . . yes,
Leo . . . but don't answer me . . . I am conceited . . .
the woman cut his leg off . . . amputated his leg . . .
in amputation . . . there is collapse . . . a damage . . .
she made mincemeat out of him . . . Godfrigh. She has
thick hair . . . Saint Mary of Egypt . . . Saint Mary's
fingers were studded with blood . . . studded—Leo, you
are my stud! And Godfrigh is dead! (LEO *grumbles*) In
Normandy we were privileged . . . and here . . . Constantinople is filled with bad air! Harm, that is what I've
had in Constantinople. Godfrigh's body is stiff now . . .
his one leg is probably quite stiff . . . fantastic! Godfrigh
drooled for the woman . . . one day I'll be toothless and
I'll drool—and then I'll remember how Godfrigh drooled
for a woman—not me—an Eastern woman—a saint . . .
perhaps then, without my teeth . . . I will be sweeter and
gentler. It's vexing—hot, false Constantinople . . . we
were deceived. Godfrigh's body will decay . . . the worms
—the parasitic worms will be full of his blood—maybe
wine—he drank a lot of wine. (*To* LEO) Worms will drink
his wine! Mercy, lovingness, Christ—give mercy and lovingness to Godfrigh—I never did. (*Crying*) Leo, will you
go with me to Normandy? I want you!

LEO   I can't.

ALICE   You must! I need you! A husband . . .

LEO   You'll get a husband again . . . but not me.

ALICE Don't you love me?

LEO No, my Alice . . . no. (*Wisely*) And you don't care.

ALICE Yes—I do—I do!

LEO No, you don't.

ALICE You're right . . . I don't . . . You wouldn't be happy in Normandy—you would be full of sorrow there . . . like I am here in Constantinople—it made us greedy —gold everywhere—in hot Constantinople—they even make Christ's eyes gold! Ecstasy . . . blood poison . . . it's all here—why do you want to stay, Leo?

LEO Constantinople? Because I love it. You know, Alice, you have the smoothest, silkiest skin. We have only one hour (*Laughs*) before the Saracens come.

ALICE Saracens come? This is the first time I've heard—is it true—are the Saracens coming?

LEO Unhummmm.

(*He kisses her*)

Blackout

Homo

●

HOMO *was first presented in the summer of 1966, by The LaMama Troupe in Europe, with the following cast:*

(*In order of appearance*)

ELIZABETH	Katina Mandas
FIRST WORKER	Kevin O'Connor
SECOND WORKER	Michael Warren Powell
BERNICE	Mari-Claire Charba
GELDEREN	Rob Thirkield
FIRST OFFICIAL	Kevin O'Connor
SECOND OFFICIAL	Michael Warren Powell
HORSE-MAN	Victor LiPari

Music and direction by Tom O'Horgan

LIST OF CHARACTERS

ELIZABETH: Ordinary woman in her
                                 fifties; a little fleshy.

FIRST WORKER, SECOND WORKER: Sturdy, proletarian
                                 types.

BERNICE:	Blonde and beautiful goddess, ego-ideal.
GELDEREN:	Elizabeth's husband. About fifty, a little fleshy.
FIRST OFFICIAL, SECOND OFFICIAL:	So-called Asiatics. Alpine or Mediterranean types.
HORSE-MAN:	Average-looking, beaten-down type.

"The most popular of the racial theories of western civilization is that which sets upon a pedestal the xanthotrichous, glaucopian, dolichocephalic variety of homo leucodermaticus, called by some the Nordic man and by Nietzsche 'the blond beast.'"

—Toynbee

ACT ONE

•

SCENE 1

The stage is dimly lit. ELIZABETH, *archetypal woman in her fifties, wears a plain black skirt and aqua blouse, white sweat-socks and brown oxfords. She crawls around on her hands and knees. Two dark, sturdy construction workers carry pails of sand and make threatening motions at her.*

ELIZABETH (*Helplessly*) I'm not free from harm. They want sand in my mouth and all my other open parts. (*Places her hands over her rear end protectively*) So that now and then I will not speak. They hinder me—O Gelderen!

(ELIZABETH *gives a long shriek*)

FIRST WORKER It'll be more than hinderin'. I'll make you kiss my Calabrese ass. You make my flesh grind.

ELIZABETH You make my flesh grind away from the bone. You shame me so. Gelderen! Gelderen!

(ELIZABETH *sobs*)

SECOND WORKER What're you copying him for? (*He shouts*) And stop crying about Gelderen!

FIRST WORKER Did she copy me?

SECOND WORKER Yeah, she said you make her flesh grind away from the bone, and that's what you said.

FIRST WORKER (*To* ELIZABETH) So you copy me, huh? You want Gelderen, huh? (*Kicks her and screams at her*) I hope you die and stink finally—I hope you just let go, like pus from a sore!

(ELIZABETH *cries and falls on her face*)

SECOND WORKER She's something ugly.

ELIZABETH (*Pathetic, screaming*) Please watch my feelings —please watch *my feelings*—I'm a European woman. My hips are much broader than a primitive woman's.

FIRST WORKER (*Jumping up and down, holding his front*) Sooo wide, sooo wiiideee—yeah, her pelvis bone's wide! ooowowoo! Sooo wiiidddee insiiideee!

ELIZABETH It's got to be—so fine human beings can be born—fine human beings with good craniums. Don't make me cry too much, it's not good for me. Oooo, please let me stand up!

SECOND WORKER You can squat.

FIRST WORKER Yeh, yeh, make her squat! I like to see a motherly-looking woman squat.

(*Laughs while* ELIZABETH *awkwardly squats*)

SECOND WORKER (*To* ELIZABETH) Finish what you were saying about craniums.

FIRST WORKER Yeh, yeh, I like that word. Craniums craniums hot fat plums who wants to see my plums. (*Chants this and makes smacking sounds*) Elizabeth, aren't my plums superior to the coney primitive's?

SECOND WORKER Well—tell him!

ELIZABETH   Yes, just as good and constant as the primitive's. But your brains are much better, and that's more important than plums, yes that's what counts, craniums. Oooo, it's so painful to squat.

FIRST WORKER (*Evilly*)   Squat or die! You just stay there squatted to the ground or else!

SECOND WORKER   Yeh—or else!

FIRST WORKER   All right, tell us more history. We won't clog you up with sand, you can speak.

ELIZABETH   Good—but can I get on my knees, please? I can't keep squatting like this. My legs are so cramped.

SECOND WORKER   All right—on your knees.

FIRST WORKER (*Screams*)   How am I gonna get my kicks if you let her stop squatting, huh?

SECOND WORKER   Look—she's going to tell us the *history*, right? So, she wants to kneel, let her kneel this time. While she's kneeling you can make believe she's squatting. Use that head of yours, cranium, remember?

FIRST WORKER (*Laughs*)   Do I! Plums plums sugar bums and plums.

SECOND WORKER   Now get her the red kneeling stool and the sexy stockings—she must look rich and powerful. She was Gelderen's woman!

FIRST WORKER   Yeh, yeh. (*He goes to the back of the stage and returns with a stool and stockings.* ELIZABETH *sits down heavily and grins, stretches her legs out and puts on the stockings*) Here y'are.

ELIZABETH   Ohhh, what a relief just to stretch my legs.

FIRST WORKER (*Screams*) You get on that kneeling stool but quick—or I'll stretch you!

SCENE 2

The front of the stage is well lit. A man stands with his hands propped on a bookcase, his back in a horizontal position. He is wearing an ordinary, shabby suit. BERNICE, *a lovely well-dressed lady, straddles him. He makes horse movements;* BERNICE *hits, spurs him, scolds and caresses.* ELIZABETH *and the workers watch from the shadows in the rear of the stage.*

ELIZABETH See, she's the superior one. (*The workers laugh*) She makes him carry on that way three and four times a day—though he loves every minute of it.

FIRST WORKER Cheez, what a sight!

ELIZABETH Indeed. But he loves it, like I say. I'll make her a bit more ruthless.

BERNICE (*Pushing the* HORSE-MAN *harder, shrieking*) Call me your goddess—you ape! Tell me how much you adore me!

HORSE-MAN My goddess—you are my goddess—I adore you!

BERNICE (*Shrieking*) Then why aren't you wearing your hump? It makes my own perfection so much more wonderful!

FIRST WORKER It gives her bliss to see him this way—with his hump-bump.

ELIZABETH (*Hysterical*) Watch her who masters, watch her who masters!

HORSE-MAN (*He is shaky, sweaty, excited*) You took my hump away because of pity.

BERNICE That's right—I gave you pity.

ELIZABETH Notice how he wants pity now and then. It makes him forget his stinking luck.

FIRST WORKER I don't know if he's that unlucky—the woman's a beauty!

ELIZABETH Yes, she is. And notice how dazzling fair she is. Must've come from the north . . . hmmm, you don't think he's got stinking luck then?

FIRST WORKER (*Excitedly*) She, the gorgeous one, might be making him go the right direction. He probably lost his faith and he knows that she could drive him back to it. Her shining shining skin!

(FIRST WORKER *makes orgiastic sounds*)

BERNICE Do you smell and hear the adulation of me? Do likewise, swine!

HORSE-MAN (*Crying*) Your beautiful, beautiful anger.

BERNICE (*Screaming*) Again! Again! And I'll tell you my rules!

HORSE-MAN (*Snorting, slobbering*) Your beautiful, beautiful anger.

ELIZABETH Her rules are *grand*. Gelderen knew them by rote!

BERNICE Sympathize and live raptly! Gossip goodly! Do not be disgraceful! Be shy! Don't vex each other! Others do not vex! Remember Christ's point of view was not vexing! Say me, enjoy the day! Say me, Lord Lord bless ye!

ELIZABETH Her blessings come in so handy—even the littlest of them.

BERNICE Hallelujah! Say me, du fit und slit go away from me!

ELIZABETH Sometimes it sounds like a foreign tongue.

BERNICE Say me, happiness of Lebanon! Say me, skin of love! Say me, arr arr and go below! Say me, refuse an evil eye! Say me, domineer the animals! Say me, match me who masters! Match me who masters! Say me more on other sabbaths! Say me again and again match me who masters! Match me who masters!

(*The* HORSE-MAN *is jubilant; the workers stomp their feet and clap hands*)

FIRST WORKER You beautiful glory!

SECOND WORKER You gray-eyed rose of heaven!

ELIZABETH She's a glorious reflection of us indeed, indeed.

BERNICE What bulky slob wants to worship me? Come ugliness!

ELIZABETH (*To the workers*) Don't go near her, slobs. You're not good enough yet!

FIRST WORKER Don't you call us names, Elizabeth. We'll use you for fertilizer!

SECOND WORKER (*Screaming*) More, goddess, scorn us more! Bring fear, bring fear!

BERNICE I am a miracle from a powerful tribe—I make alive the question of life! I stir it up like mosquitoes. Who urges me on?

FIRST WORKER (*Screaming*) I do! I do! Goddess, goddess, let me grovel before you—let me give you my skin, my eyes, my teeth!

208

ELIZABETH (*Mocks him*)   All of him, why don't you take all of him, hair to ankle joints—the whole slob, Bernice!

FIRST WORKER (*To* ELIZABETH)   I swear you're gonna be shoved in the ground! I'm not a slob! We put those stockings on you, let your knees rest on a rich stool? Don't forget! (*He screams*) Bernice, kick me, kick me, rule me, rule me!

BERNICE   My pubis is *silken,* thou swine! Thou hast come from a bulky cotton cunt, thou and I are far apart!

(*The* HORSE-MAN *becomes angry and flips* BERNICE *off his back.* BERNICE *stands before him and gently strokes his face*)

FIRST WORKER   Did she say what I thought she said?

BERNICE   Calm, be calm. 'Tweren't a really naughty word. I am still thy blessed mistress who governs thee!

SECOND WORKER   I believe she said that your mother has a cotton cunt.

ELIZABETH   Bernice, Bernice—you're not ever supposed to use that kind of word! Too *common.* A goddess is never, ever common. These men don't understand your poetic perceptions—they can only see the upper parts, never the bottom.

BERNICE   I am your goddess and your executioner. My wrath waxes hot! (*Screaming*) I said the word "punt," which is an African land known for its perfumes!

FIRST WORKER   Yeah, yeah—we heard what you said and it weren't the name of an African land!

SECOND WORKER   You said "cotton cunt"!

ELIZABETH   Now, now, she did not. She said "punt," which is the ancient name for Somaliland.

FIRST WORKER   We probably did hear wrong.

SECOND WORKER   So we heard wrong, yeah. Please get back on the man again.

(BERNICE *straddles the* HORSE-MAN *again and rides him harder than ever. The workers and* ELIZABETH *cheer*)

SCENE 3

In the court of the Asiatics. Under the Asiatic rule, the Dutch are allowed the privilege of doing their business at the price of self-abasement. It's the year 1852. GELDEREN *is being humiliated by two officials.* GELDEREN *is stolid, fair and fat. The Asiatics are not necessarily Mongol-looking—Mediterranean types are fine. Their English is perfect;* GELDEREN's *very poor.*

GELDEREN   I vant to be shuckcessful, das ist all. In my oon country—can't! I'm here—your fool. So here I go.

(GELDEREN *acts as ridiculous as possible; the officials watch, superior and pleased*)

FIRST OFFICIAL   Blow air out of your nose, please. I feel joy when I see that. O you red fish, O you red fish.

(FIRST OFFICIAL *laughs*)

GELDEREN   Thank God, my mutter's dead.

(GELDEREN *blows air out of his nose*)

SECOND OFFICIAL   Your mother, dead? O—too bad. Curse her!

GELDEREN   Nein. But vy?

210

FIRST OFFICIAL (*Screaming*)   Curse! Curse! Curse your mother's smoke!

GELDEREN (*Whines*)   My mutter don't smoke.

SECOND OFFICIAL (*Laughs*)   Smoke, smoke—he said his mother don't smoke. Your mother's a smoked and roasted fish!

FIRST OFFICIAL   Let's make the fish pretend he's skidding on shit!

   (FIRST OFFICIAL *laughs*)

SECOND OFFICIAL   Yes, sir, very good. Red fish, you skid on shit now. And curse, curse your mother!

GELDEREN   But vat do I say? I'm a businessman, a trader. Not a defiler. (*Skids, blows air, farts*) So—maybe I emberresh mineself some. So, these people hev a sense of humor.

FIRST OFFICIAL (*Cups his hands to his mouth and screams*) You're not skidding! Come on you, you shit-skid!

SECOND OFFICIAL   And curse your whore mother!

GELDEREN   My mutter, you're a whore—I don't vant extreme poverty—so mother you a whore! I'm here—my heart has gotta be a block of stone—I vant the living!

FIRST OFFICIAL   Pink legs, be funnier, funnier!

SECOND OFFICIAL   You say a block of stone. (*He screams*) Call your mother's ghost a block of stone that you wipe your shit-feet on! Do it, do it!

GELDEREN (*Falls on the floor, blubbering*)   I wipe my feet-shit on you, Mamma. I wipe my feet . . .

FIRST OFFICIAL   Come off it! You're here for the money. Don't get sentimental.

SECOND OFFICIAL Hollander, make me laugh! I want to laugh!

GELDEREN (*Gets up and dances*) I'll sing, I'll sing.

FIRST OFFICIAL Sing—sing red fish—sing and fool for us. You Western pig!

SECOND OFFICIAL Blow air out of your nose and fart and skid and skid and skid!

GELDEREN (*Singly sadly*) I'm craving money money money for my bread. I'll hev enough money money money in mine bed, und das is vy I here.

(GELDEREN *ends the song high and sad. The officials are doubled over with laughter*)

SECOND OFFICIAL You're not skidding!

FIRST OFFICIAL (*To* SECOND OFFICIAL) Did you like that song?

SECOND OFFICIAL So so.

FIRST OFFICIAL I'm not sure I liked it.

SECOND OFFICIAL Well—let him sing another.

FIRST OFFICIAL Sing one about your wife! Gelderen, your wife!

(FIRST OFFICIAL *laughs*)

SECOND OFFICIAL Yes, one about your wife. The big thing with the blinded eyes—I romped on her yesterday!

FIRST OFFICIAL Naw, she's not blinded—just without a healthy color. (*Screaming*) Light-eyed inferior female! Eyes without a healthy color!

GELDEREN (*Simpers*) In mine country, Elizabeth's eyes are called beautiful. Light, light-blue eyes like a gless of vater.

FIRST OFFICIAL (*Laughs*) His wife's eyes beautiful. Our eyes are beautiful, especially our women's!

SECOND OFFICIAL Gay black eyes, merry-looking, flirty.

FIRST OFFICIAL His saying that his wife's eyes are beautiful really means that he believes our women's eyes are unbeautiful!

GELDEREN No. No. They're different from each other, that's all. Black, blue, they both see!

FIRST OFFICIAL (*Screaming*) Our women's eyes unbeautiful! I resent it! I resent it! You shall run a foot race now and scream out how you welcome having your whole race annihilated!

SECOND OFFICIAL (*Screaming*) Your women's skins are red and hairy like the filthy Ainu. You are brothers of the primitive Ainu animals. Run, run, Hollander animal. (*He sighs and breathes heavily*) Oooo, my just hatred exhausts me.

FIRST OFFICIAL Hollander, run the foot race! And sing praises to us, your masters!

GELDEREN (*Running back and forth, he sings*) O my soul, my saviour come to me how great thou art how great thou art.

FIRST OFFICIAL (*Disgusted*) O now stop!

SECOND OFFICIAL Leave!

FIRST OFFICIAL (*A bit pleasant*) See you next year.

SECOND OFFICIAL (*Smiling*)   Call us your gods before you go.

GELDEREN   You are my gods.

(GELDEREN *exits*)

SCENE 4

The present. ELIZABETH *is dressed elegantly. She sits, legs wide apart like a Hindu dancer, on a fancy chair made to look like a throne. The workers are on their knees before her.*

FIRST WORKER (*Imploring*)   Oppress us, listen to us!

SECOND WORKER   Defend us, you goddess!

FIRST WORKER   Make me stop kicking with my hind legs. O help me, help!

(*Both men thrash around in repulsive servitude*)

SECOND WORKER   Protect us like you protect the Fetus. O don't be mean. For why are you mean?

FIRST WORKER   Give us a reason. Our hearts are up to you!

SECOND WORKER   Gives us the milk from you. Let us sleep near your thighs!

FIRST WORKER   So white, so white!

SECOND WORKER   Yes, white, white, white. (*Screaming*) O cup us in your maternal hands!

FIRST WORKER   There's an itch on my skin! (*Screaming*) O skin us, mother! Stack our bones up in a pile!

ELIZABETH   When I take the marrow out, it won't be black. 'Twill be gold-colored!

FIRST WORKER   O pack us back like we were once!

SECOND WORKER   Make us be perfect!

ELIZABETH   I'll heal thy sores in my *own* good time.

FIRST WORKER   Give us the test!

SECOND WORKER   (*Giggles*)   O yes, the test! The test!

(*Both workers laugh crazily*)

ELIZABETH   All right, the test.

FIRST WORKER   I'll get the steel.

(*He exits and comes back with a steel bar. He places it center stage*)

SECOND WORKER   Go ahead, Elizabeth. Go ahead!

ELIZABETH   (*Rising, queen-like*)   Thou art all unconfident. Do you fathom that? You fools! You shoe! You heaven! You have had affairs of the heart. Fathom that?

SECOND WORKER   The part about the sores, the sores!

ELIZABETH   Thou art *women!* So, if thou art women, tie a stick onto thy feminine part. It can cause a goodly pleasure too. It's valid but cannot cause a birth. But neither can you receive a sore from it—but you cannot bring forth a fruit from it either! Put some water on the steel! (*They sprinkle water on the bar*) Lick that hard steel! (*Workers crawl and lick the bar*) Do you like it? (*Workers nod frantically and lick the steel*) Pretend that it's pieces of trout. Is the liking of it generating in you? Now put your mono-major part on trout and troutize on it! (*Workers sweep their arms from pelvis to bar, lick etc.*) Thy filth is gone and thy sores are cured!

(*Workers sprawl out, satisfied*)

FIRST WORKER This is so much better than intercourse, sometimes.

SECOND WORKER Sometimes this is better, yes, yeh, yes.

FIRST WORKER But ooh Bernice. 'Member Bernice?

SECOND WORKER I would give her my cranium—if I could touch Bernice's head. If she wanted it!

FIRST WORKER Her long legs, her blonde eyebrows. I wasn't able to breathe—she was so beautiful.

SECOND WORKER (*Turns suddenly to* ELIZABETH, *who looks uncomfortable*) You are a hiss from the bowels!

FIRST WORKER She is! You're right! It's true! Elizabeth's just a bad-smelling female!

SECOND WORKER (*To* ELIZABETH, *screaming*) What happened, you boiled chicken!

FIRST WORKER (*Screaming*) What happened to us?

ELIZABETH (*Pathetic, repulsive*) It's hard, so hard . . . Bernice was so perfect . . . the veins in my legs are so full of blood, they hurt so. Let me put them together, please.

FIRST WORKER (*Screaming*) O close them, close them! Now tell us why you let those Asiatics trump us, triumph over us! Why they were allowed to weaken us!
    (FIRST WORKER *rushes at* ELIZABETH *and starts to pull her off the chair, but* SECOND WORKER *pulls him back*)

SECOND WORKER Cool down, cool down, you fanatic. I feel exactly the way you do—but she is all we have!

    (SECOND WORKER *points his finger at* ELIZABETH)

ELIZABETH The Asiatics crunched our strength up with

216

their teeth . . . they raped and stole our best blood! They left their blood in us. Their stinking pissy blood in us to yellow up our skins and make our eyes black! We were once all rosy and fair as Bernice.

FIRST WORKER (*Stands proud*) You mean I was once fair-haired and and gray-eyed?

SECOND WORKER And powerfully built?

ELIZABETH (*Shouting*) Yes, yes, for we came from the North!

FIRST WORKER And where did the Asiatics come from?

ELIZABETH (*Shouting*) From the South the South the South! The hot wearying South! We exchanged our gods for their evil and falsity. They took our divinity and gave us their intestinal tracts!

FIRST WORKER I knew I had a good reason for being bitter. We were once really great!

SECOND WORKER Fantastic!

ELIZABETH The women were fascinating, the soil tilled, the trees flowering. We kissed each other's beautiful lips.

FIRST WORKER Not the blooming asses of the Asiatics!

ELIZABETH Gelderen helped end our purity, because of his greed . . . I know it. It was his fault. O he was completely vile!

SECOND WORKER You're always blaming Gelderen!

FIRST WORKER Yeah . . . it's always Gelderen's fault . . . (*Mimicking*) It was his fault . . . the Asiatics put the bite on him. Took his vigor away. And you, you bitch, couldn't stop being raped by them!

ELIZABETH How could I? I had no protector. O stop it now! Everything will be all right! (*She puts her fingers in a*

glass) There's sugar on my fingers . . . here have some
. . . (*They suck her fingers*) Now isn't that nice, sweet?
A tiger is sweet . . . we were once tigers. Our lips and
tongues were covered with jewels. (*She keeps sticking
her fingers into the glass, then into their mouths*) Here,
more. This is as nice as licking the steel . . . not one
among us was evil. (*Hums*) Five five five five five Xavier
Xavier and Valhalla and the Mongols and the Mongols
and the Mongols may not enter our holy place for they
eat of the dog's body and are lightless . . . five five five
five five . . .

Blackout

ACT TWO

●

SCENE 1

BERNICE *sits on the throne-chair, combing and preening.
The* HORSE-MAN *is dressed like a peasant. He is humpbacked
now. He waits on her, handing her combs, brushing her
clothes, etc.*

BERNICE (*Stretching*) My shrewdness can't be beaten. Not
once have I ever made a false squeeze. I'm a prime mammal. Isn't that so?

HORSE-MAN You're the greatest! Sweet and gentle.

BERNICE I am health and beauty! Even when I lose my
teeth, I shall never make a false squeeze.

HORSE-MAN You cure my blood-poison.

BERNICE When I want to. (*Sits down; the* HORSE-MAN *takes
her stockings off*) Bring the pumice stone. I must get rid
of these calluses. (*He shuffles off to get a pumice stone,
comes back and kneels before her and files her heels*)
Gentle, gentle.

HORSE-MAN I think my hands stain your feet.

BERNICE O . . . it's all right.

HORSE-MAN But my blood-poison. Thou art so fair, so fair.

219

(BERNICE *runs her foot through his hair*)

BERNICE   It makes thee happy to serve me, doesn't it?

(*She smiles gently*)

HORSE-MAN   Very happy.

BERNICE   Thou dost not ask an explanation for thy deformity?

HORSE-MAN   No. I know the reason. (*Laughs*) I love you when your hair is down. When you are not too cruel.

BERNICE   You are banal!

(*She laughs*)

HORSE-MAN (*Laughs*)   It is our way.

BERNICE   You are a moron with an infection!

HORSE-MAN   I have ulcers all over me. I'm at odds and ends with myself!

BERNICE   A disgusting infection that works itself out of your tongue!

HORSE-MAN   Everything you say I take to my head and heart!

BERNICE (*Places her foot on his face*)   I could cure your infection with a horse-laugh! Haw, haw, haw! I rib you and own you, the lousy flesh of you. . . . You look as if you suffer from eternal sunstroke.

HORSE-MAN   Vinegar and and *vinegar* ruined my body!

BERNICE (*Mocking*)   Vinegar and and vinegar ruined your body. No . . . it didn't! Thou art and always were a simple piss-slapping beast. A slavish lunatic! Lay down and be inferior!

HORSE-MAN   You mean I'm not now, when I stand?

BERNICE Lay down and be inferior! (*She laughs as he lies down*) Stand up and be inferior! (*He stands up*) See, you are inferior when you lay down and stand up! Say that you have a rupture!

HORSE-MAN I have a rupture.

BERNICE Nod your head! And say that you have a rupture again.

HORSE-MAN (*Nodding*) I have a rupture.

BERNICE Where, where? Where is the rupture? (*Screaming*) Where are you ruptured?

HORSE-MAN I don't know.

BERNICE In the soul, in the body . . . simple as that. (*Shouting*) Say in the soul, in the body you are ruptured! Say that your soul and body are ruptured!

HORSE-MAN (*Shouting*) In the soul, in the body I am ruptured. My soul and body are ruptured!

BERNICE I domineer you with a finger and you nod your head quickly—no—it was not the fault of vinegar that you have a rupture, blood-poison and a hump!

HORSE-MAN I know the reason—it was the invasion. The Asiatics divided and conquered us.

BERNICE (*Screaming*) No—it was not the Asiatic invasion! You fat intestine! You gloomy crack-pot! You piece of dirty albumin!

HORSE-MAN (*Falling at her feet*) O—please don't be so very angry! (*Crying*) Queen, goddess, I fear you, I fear you.

BERNICE (*Looking at him indifferently*) I feel like dozing. You irk my nervous system. I want to doze. (*Yawns*) You will know the reason one day. I shall doze . . . your

Queen has a natural appetite for sleep . . . it is good to be healthy . . . never let your eyes off me and you will become healthy . . . we care for our own.

(BERNICE *falls asleep. He stands watching her, his finger in his mouth.* ELIZABETH's *voice is heard offstage saying "five" over and over again. This should be said long and drawn out, like an old lady's croaky voice*)

ELIZABETH'S VOICE   five five five five five . . .

BERNICE (*Awakens*) She's doing that again. (*Shivers*) Why does she do that horrid ritual? It puts a bitter lump in my heart.

ELIZABETH'S VOICE   five five five five five . . .

HORSE-MAN   It's her bad manners. A private sexual gimmick that she does with the slobs.

ELIZABETH'S VOICE   five five five five five . . .

BERNICE   O, a gimmick, huh. Maybe they suck her fingers instead of her breasts. Let me ponder about that a bit. They suck her—her fingers. Is that it?

HORSE-MAN   I don't know—I'm not sure.

BERNICE   Sucking her fingers—I'll bet that's it. O—but it makes me nervous. (*Shouting*) How dare she wake me from my doze—unhealthy pervert, unhealthy pervert!

ELIZABETH'S VOICE   five five five five five five my affliction my affliction prompt up my spirit to heavenly harmony at daybreak and evening at dearest and sweetest time save me from raging and fury.

BERNICE   What a chant . . . what a lewd chant! O, I'm not a prig. A goddess like me has flitted and gorged upon . . .

ELIZABETH'S VOICE   five five five five five . . .

HORSE-MAN They're doing something that calms their tensions. Gives them contentment.

BERNICE But she's keeping me awake! (*Shouting*) Her mucus-mouth is keeping me awake!

ELIZABETH'S VOICE five five five five five . . .

BERNICE Maybe it's not her tits—I mean fingers, maybe it's her shoes—maybe they're sucking the tips of her shoes.

HORSE-MAN (*Screaming*) Stop it, you degenerates! You are aggravating the goddess!

BERNICE (*Screaming*) I am your queen, your goddess—control yourselves! Can you not control yourselves?

ELIZABETH'S VOICE five five five five five I sing to your health a gentle frigging tune, the fair-tressed graces o roundelays of balling springtimes coming in. Thrust sickness away—uplift us the crooked-legged and savage-faced!

BERNICE She sounds as if she has the burning itch! (*Shouting*) Listen to me, Elizabeth—listen to thy queen! Thou art hateful within and without—thou art corrupt and I can do nothing! Just love me until you die!

HORSE-MAN She's right, Elizabeth—you have no choice—you're black rot!

BERNICE (*Puts her hands on the* HORSE-MAN's *head*) Who practices lunacy, we or they?

ELIZABETH'S VOICE five five five five five . . .

SCENE 2

In Asia. ELIZABETH *and* GELDEREN *are wearing simple clothes. She is dressed as in the first act.*

ELIZABETH Let's remind ourselves, Gelderen, that we are being penalized—you act sometimes as if it were a joke!

GELDEREN Whose gonna gif us bread to fry? (*Shouting*) I gotta make a living. I have so far a lot of money—and here I made it. Anyway, it's not too bad.

ELIZABETH I have been raped by the Asiatics!

GELDEREN I know. And *that* I don't like. It's a shame that they should . . .

ELIZABETH Well—what are you going to do about it?

GELDEREN I'm not a shining knight and I'm not a sorehead and I'm not a wizard! I can't use my hands both for making a buck and stopping you from being assaulted.

ELIZABETH But our blood must be pure!

GELDEREN (*Embraces her*) Yes—and nobody's such a pureblood like you—let's . . .

ELIZABETH (*Pushing him off*) You've got hold of the wrong end of the stick!

224

GELDEREN (*Laughs*) So—you tek hold of the right end.

ELIZABETH You fool! As long as our blood remains pure our civilization goes from strength to strength! But, but it's being diluted—our race is being weakened.

(ELIZABETH *weeps*)

GELDEREN Listen, we are not down and out. Stop being unhappy. You too serious. Laugh a little, Elizabeth, laugh.

ELIZABETH (*Screaming*) Your grandchildren will curse you!

GELDEREN So, I'll curse the black-eyed defils back. Anyvay, they'll be educated, a little more liberal. Maybe they von't curse me.

ELIZABETH You have done this for money! (*Throwing her arms around and storming*) Do you realize that, for money! You have sold Hedin down the river! Egil down the river! All our bold warriors down the river! Our tall, gray-eyed warriors. All down the river! You mock our gods!

GELDEREN You forgot about Keldur!

ELIZABETH Yes—Keldur too! You're going to give them— our grandchildren, great-grandchildren, gout, cataract and liver trouble. There won't be heroes any more.

(ELIZABETH *weeps*)

GELDEREN (*Trying to embrace her*) You get me so hot for you ven you start talking about our racial purity. All I vant to do is . . .

ELIZABETH (*Shouting*) You deserve a scourging! You should be beaten up!

GELDEREN Listen, I have enough from the stinky Asiatics! I don't need it from you. I vant a little love from you—

a little sympathy—a little sex. Don't exhaust me with your
talk.

ELIZABETH   Mark my words! Our descendants will remember us and weep! They'll punish us as they punish themselves! They'll hate each other. Hate each other's bodies!
Each other's minds! And all because they'll know they
look stupid standing next to all those marble statues!

GELDEREN   You are hungry. Here, let me mek you a boiled
banana sandwich. You'll feel better.

ELIZABETH   (*Screaming*)   I don't want to eat Asiatic food!
The monkey's food!

GELDEREN   (*Irritated*)   Eat a roast ox, if you can find one.
I can't find one.

ELIZABETH   We came from the North, from the North.
Everybody who was anybody came from the *North!*

GELDEREN   Yeah—and they froze their tits. That's why they
vent South! Listen, it's inevitable that ve hev contact with
people, vith the Asiatics. You can't escape it. But keep
the nice memories if you vant to. But don't let it make
you sick! Lots of things lead up to our migrations. Ve
clashed vith our own people. Some, some vere good, some
vere bad. Dere's good und bad in all people. Ill-feeling
vas transmitted to our kinsmen. It'll be transmitted to
our descendants. (*Shouting*) Everybody vill be involved.
It's inevitable.

ELIZABETH   And death will result! It'll be the end—and
that's inevitable—but it's your choice, not mine. We'll
not rule beautiful lands any more; just burying ground!
We'll lay our bodies over it. The Asiatics will haul our
corpses away with their teeth! We'll have bite marks and
fungus on us. They'll scatter us in a circle like shit.

GELDEREN You are alvays a morbid person—and alvays quarreling with me! There vas no other vay for me to make a living! That's vy I'm here!

ELIZABETH You have guided us and finished us! You've chewed us up! Our descendants will have no health, no vigor, no praise from their world in their time. They'll be cripples! They'll rave at each other! They'll be disobedient . . . just a fat bunch of rottenness . . . their virtue dead long ago. They'll look for rulers from another race, greedy rulers who will flatter them, the vilest of them. Rulers who will remind them of their ancient nobility. For their rulers will all be fair-haired and light-eyed, and the majority of them that serve will be as dark and as ugly as monkeys! Their enslavement to the physically superior type will be universally approved by public opinion! And it's your doing. All yours!

GELDEREN Plato's politics—poop! You hev a crazy imagination! First of all, they von't be so dark and ugly as you say. Next you are a racial crackpot, concerned only with the physical und never with a little common-sense. You know the Asiatics hev a pretty good thing going on! Lottsa nice statues, nice rugs, nice literature, nice preparation of food . . .

ELIZABETH They are sensual! They are feminine in their desire for luxury. They lack strength, discipline . . .

GELDEREN They sure are disciplining me all the time.

(GELDEREN *rubs his back in pain*)

ELIZABETH They are cruel barbarians! Nobody is as cruel as an Asiatic.

GELDEREN Ve hev made mincemeat out of the faces of foreignors too, you know. There have been baby-ears in our lunch boxes and unborn children on the end of our long swords. Ve're a pretty cruel folks too, you know.

ELIZABETH (*Shouting*) There's a difference! There's a difference! We are us! And they are them! Ours was always a noble and honorable victory over inferior peoples. Theirs is a savage and barbaric attack on civilization! They are a tribe! We are a nation!

GELDEREN I don' care vat you say—you chauvinist! I stay here vere the excitement is! The money too! Tribe, nation, different names for the same thing. And also the Asiatics say the same thing—that theirs is the noble struggle. That theirs is the virtuous triumph over inferiors. So let's try to do the best ve can under the circumstances and if a coupla grafts on our different trees are made—their color eyes on my face, I mean, on my child's or grandchild's face, and my color hair on their child's or grandchild's head, so vat's so veird about it or bad about it? I say live und let live.

ELIZABETH They make you behave so indecently! They humiliate you so. It disgusts me to see you so servile to them!

GELDEREN Look at it the other vay. You could admire my tenacity vith vhich I hold my ground and mek my money year in and year out. Das is the real fiber of your precious blond beast. That is a man! I can stomach the intolerable conditions like a tiger can stomach a rotten goat ven he's hungry! Yes—ven he's hungry! I a real strong man! Ven they mek me cut capers for them and ven they make me get drunk—by forcing me to drink, so that I am a living demonstration to their young of vat drunkenness looks like, I think to myself—I am a man! A strong man and I can stomach anything for a gain. And don't you forget I gain! Ve gain! In my belly I can hold a lot of indignation—so long as I get my lunch also. And dis is not the first time such a thing is done. No. It vas also done by our noble ancestors ven they vere traders in a foreign land. So, it's nothing new.

ELIZABETH I know now that I have the heaviest burden. You've rooted me to this earth. I am exhaling my breath into this unclean land. You're making my spirit thin and poor. I'll be a slave yet. I know it. You won't protect me.

SCENE 3

A polka record is playing; the two workers are dancing around. ELIZABETH *is on her hands and knees, watching.*

FIRST WORKER (*Singing*) Backward and forward I go ookee Kachki ping ping.

SECOND WORKER (*Singing*) With a passion in my belly and I'm crooning unlike Bing.

(SECOND WORKER *laughs*)

FIRST WORKER (*Singing*) Come here, you, and call me by my native name ding ding—the rest of you too fat to dance my pliant dance of majesty. (FIRST WORKER *laughs. This last part of the song is sung by both workers*) How is this, Elizabeth. Isn't it better?

ELIZABETH (*Clapping*) It was a good dance. You don't look foolish at all. You do it much better.

FIRST WORKER (*Stops dancing*) The lady's not wrong! We do it much better.

(FIRST WORKER *kicks* ELIZABETH)

SECOND WORKER I say the same thing. The lady is not wrong! We do it much better!

(SECOND WORKER *kicks her*)

ELIZABETH You shame me so.

(ELIZABETH *weeps. Both workers dance around her, singing*)

WORKERS (*Singing together*) O exalted and sublime woman, kala, kala, kala.

ELIZABETH You should dig my grave instead of mocking me!

FIRST WORKER Listen, you. You just shut up and sit cross-legged!

SECOND WORKER That's right. Sit cross-legged!

ELIZABETH (*Sits cross-legged*) You have no pity for me! You shame me so! You won't even let me have a clean dress! This one is so foul.

FIRST WORKER (*Mimicking*) This one is so foul. (*Shouting*) One dress is enough for any woman!

SECOND WORKER Yeh, some women don't wear any clothes at all. (*They laugh*) Not even a cloth during their menses!

FIRST WORKER Yeh, the savages do that. We'll let you wash your dress one day.

SECOND WORKER Tomorrow you can wash it, Elizabeth. You'll be clean then—you'll be sexy—wow wow. You'll look like you have no faults at all!

FIRST WORKER What're you promising her? She is our mother (*He pronounces it "mowthra"*) not our girl friend.

SECOND WORKER Are you crazy? She isn't our mowthra!

FIRST WORKER I know it. But I say it anyway. Mowthra! Mowthra!

ELIZABETH I have so many roles—for anybody's sadistic practices. O—it's all so . . .

FIRST WORKER O, listen, would you rather be the emperor of the Orient or our mowthra? Or an orangutan showing your ass off?

FIRST WORKER and SECOND WORKER O orangutan you've no shame you show your ass, seeds and nuts!

SECOND WORKER Don't you complain! Sometimes when you wear the stockings, we feel that you are our goddess!

FIRST WORKER A living goddess.

ELIZABETH I make alive the question of life!

SECOND WORKER Yeh, yeh—that's just what Elizabeth said to the horse-man.

FIRST WORKER You mean Bernice said it to the horse-man!

SECOND WORKER That's right. I mean Bernice! What a mistake. Terrible mistake! Confusing Elizabeth with Bernice!

ELIZABETH I've pulled mandrakes out of the ground by their roots! Fat and tender mandrakes!

FIRST WORKER I wonder if Bernice ever pulled on a fat and tender mandrake?

SECOND WORKER What I would love to see is a contest between Bernice and Elizabeth—a mandrake-pulling contest! Whoever makes the little guy scream first is the winner.

(SECOND WORKER *laughs*)

FIRST WORKER Bernice would win.

SECOND WORKER Probably. I mean definitely! Gee—they grow from spilled seed!

FIRST WORKER Spilled seed?

SECOND WORKER Yeah—sperm fallen on the ground. Spilled seed sounds so pretty though . . . spilled seed.

FIRST WORKER Yeah, it's a pleasant sound . . . makes me feel dreamy. Why O why did our genitals all have to turn to meat und fat—like capons!

SECOND WORKER Why do you say meat und fat? Why don't you just say meat and fat!

ELIZABETH (*Screaming*) He's imitating Gelderen!

SECOND WORKER Were you really imitating Gelderen?

FIRST WORKER Hmmmmmmhmmm, spilled seed. . . . (*Shouting*) I don't know if I was imitating Gelderen!

SECOND WORKER Well—we were related! A contest between Bernice and Elizabeth. I like that idea.

ELIZABETH Well—I don't! It would be sacrilegious! Me—a lowly woman—in a contest with Bernice! Her radiance would blind us all!

FIRST WORKER Listen—now don't tear yourself down!

SECOND WORKER Yeh, we'll do it for you when we want to. Elizabeth, get Bernice here and fill this place up with mandrakes!

FIRST WORKER We have no seed that we can spill. Our whole reproductive system turned to meat und fat. But we have Elizabeth and Elizabeth can make the flowers and the mandrakes grow!

ELIZABETH (*Weepy*) It's not a good idea. Something will

233

happen and you'll blame me. You'll insult me and do worse things.

FIRST WORKER   Nothing'll happen—you do this for us!

ELIZABETH   But you say that Bernice can win—positively. I know that she can also. There is just no point.

FIRST WORKER   (*Kicks her and shouts*)   Get Bernice!

SECOND WORKER   (*Shouting*)   Get Bernice! Get Bernice!

ELIZABETH   (*Hysterical*)   O the Asiatics made you this way —so brutal, brutal . . .

FIRST WORKER   (*Kicks her*)   Mandrake-pulling contest. Fat and tender mandrakes. Get Bernice, get Bernice!

SECOND WORKER   (*Kicks her*)   No clean dress—no clean dress for you! We'll make you squat forever! Do you want to squat forever?

ELIZABETH   (*Crying*)   No, no, no, Bernice, Bernice, Bernice! You can't be near her because you're not good enough! You're slobs!

FIRST WORKER   You don't call us names! (*Kicks her*) I want to be near her! I'll wash—I'll wash my hands, my feet, my empty crotch! I'll be clean as a whistle for Bernice!

SECOND WORKER   Me too. I want to be near her!

ELIZABETH   But it's not right! It's never been done that way. You must only watch her while you sit in the dark. She must have all the light!

FIRST WORKER   I want the light too! I'm alive—even though I have an empty crotch! I want to share the light too.

ELIZABETH   Your virtue is dead! Gelderen ruined us all! We're miserable, miserable!

FIRST WORKER   (*Screaming*)   No we're not! You get Bernice!

SECOND WORKER (*Screaming*) Get Bernice, get Bernice!

ELIZABETH (*Frantically*) Here's my fingers. Suck on my fingers! They will calm you down. Lick my sweet fingers! Get me the glass . . . I'll get the glass . . . (*Crawls toward the glass and dips her hands into it*) Here's my fingers—lick them, they're sweet!

FIRST WORKER (*Shouting*) We want Bernice! We want you and her together!

SECOND WORKER (*Shouting*) I want your fingers, Elizabeth! I mean I want Bernice! Get Bernice! I want the light, the sweetness!

(*Workers are hunched over, crying.* ELIZABETH *crawls to them and sticks her fingers in their mouths*)

ELIZABETH (*Takes deep breaths*) Five five five five five when I scream a new race will emerge from between my thighs—the bones will be big and the heads long and thin—o for that day we wait and we will have all wokened at the same time—five five five five five five five five . . .

Blackout

About the Author

ROCHELLE OWENS was born and educated in Brooklyn, New York, and attended the Herbert Berghof Studio and The New School. Miss Owens, who is also a poet, translator, critic, and writer of short fiction, has had her work published in many of the leading magazines and journals and in several anthologies. She has published two books of poetry and has given many readings. Her plays have been produced at the Judson Poets' Theatre, the Tyrone Guthrie Theatre in Minneapolis, the Theatre of the Living Arts in Philadelphia, and by the LaMama Troupe in New York and throughout Europe.

In 1967–68, Miss Owens was awarded a fellowship in the A.B.C.-Yale School of Drama Program: Writing for the Camera. Her play *Futz* won the OBIE Best Play award for 1967. She is married and lives in New York City.